CW00660569

Key to abbreviations

AC   Accommodation crossing
ABCL   Automatic barrier crossing locally monitored
AHB   Automatic half barrier
AOCL   Automatic open crossing locally monitored
AOCR   Automatic open crossing remotely monitored
Boom   Boom gates operated from a signalbox
CCTV   Crossing monitored by closed circuit television
CKG   Gates operated by a crossing keeper
FP   Footpath crossing
MCB   Manually-controlled barriers
MG   Manned gates (worked from a signalbox)
MWL   Miniature warning lights (red and green)
MWLB   Miniature warning lights (red and green) with user-
        operated barriers
OC   Occupation crossing
R/G   Red/green lights
TMO   Gates operated by the traincrew
UWG   User-worked gates (T – with telephone)

First published 2008

ISBN (10) 0 7110 3308 0
ISBN (13) 978 0 7110 3308 5

Published by Ian Allan Publishing
an imprint of Ian Allan Publishing Ltd, Hersham,
Surrey, KT12 4RG

Printed in England by Ian Allan Publishing Ltd, Hersham,
Surrey, KT12 4RG

Code: 0811/B2

Visit the Ian Allan Publishing website at
www.ianallanpublishing.com

CONTENTS

PREFACE

Why a book on level crossings? Because they represent the last great unsolved threat of disaster still facing railways. This is not because they are becoming less safe, quite the opposite, but because one of the main causes of disaster over the centuries — drivers passing signals at danger and running into collision — has been largely (but not entirely) solved by the installation of the Train Protection and Warning System.

At level crossings there is a clash of two cultures. On one hand the well-organised operation of trains using adequately trained staff and applying properly understood railway safety principles. On the other millions of road vehicle drivers of varying degrees of competence from the properly trained and experienced long distance heavy goods driver to the latest reckless 17 year-old showing off in front of his even younger girl friends (oh, yes, the reader will find quite a few examples of those multi-fatality accidents in these pages).

The problem arose when British Railways (BR) abandoned its century-old principle of keeping responsibility for safety at level crossings within its own control. For reasons discussed in these pages BR could no longer maintain that stance and had to hand over to the road user most of the responsibility for safety (not only his own but also that of the passengers and crew in the train). To enable the road user to cross safely a variety of warning signs, bells, buzzers, lights flashing and steady, and instruction notices have been provided, but they are only effective if seen, understood and correctly acted upon, which unfortunately is not always the case as instances of accidents quoted in the book will demonstrate. And it assumes of course that the reader understands the English language in the first place. Even the unambiguous red light and the word 'Stop' is open to fatal misinterpretation apparently.

Public level crossings are only one part of the road/rail interface. Road vehicles can escape on to the railway at overbridges, through fences alongside the railway and even bursting through the fended-off end of closed roads. The railway authorities do have a degree of control of public safety at public level crossings. They have little or none at the thousands of private level crossings (often known as occupation crossings) where the crossing user is almost entirely responsible for his own safety and that of the approaching train and can drive a heavy lorry across the line whenever he chooses to do so. Telephones to a signalbox are often provided, but that is only effective if they are used, which is not always the case.

The replacement of level crossings by bridges is the only complete answer, but at a cost which in most cases is not justified by the incremental increase in safety. A definitive answer has yet to be found.

The compilation of this book has been greatly assisted by the splendid and detailed maps provided by the Quail Track Diagram company, TRACKmaps, and I wish to record my appreciation. The annual accident reports of the Railway Inspectorate and its successors have been invaluable. I would also like to record my appreciation of the help given by Alan Cooksey, a former Deputy Chief Inspecting Officer of Railways, Chris Hall, an inspector with the Railway Accidents Investigation Branch, Nigel Harris, Managing Editor of *RAIL* magazine, who showed me some of the more interesting examples of level crossings in the Peterborough area, and Bill Smith, a retired signalman, who provided many of the photographs displayed in this book.

A colleague, Peter van der Mark, who is in current railway employment, has provided Chapter 11 — An International Perspective. Peter is well-qualified to write on this subject. He is widely travelled and has an encyclopedic knowledge of the world's railways, their level crossings and the accidents which occur on them. I am deeply grateful to him for his part in this work.

Stanley Hall MBE
Chartered Fellow, Institute of Logistics and Transport
Fellow, Institution of Railway Operators
Honorary Fellow, Institution of Railway Signal Engineers
Embsay, Skipton

HOW IT ALL BEGAN

Developments up to 1863

1

Road/rail level crossings came into being when the mining of coal and the quarrying of aggregates began some distance from the place of ultimate use, requiring a form of transport from the one to the other. In an earlier age pack-horses or horse-drawn carts would have sufficed, but when mining and quarrying began on an industrial scale a more efficient and reliable form of transport was needed. The roads of the day were inadequate and in wet weather quickly became muddy and almost impassable to heavily-laden carts. The laying of simple railway tracks on what would now be termed narrow gauge provided the answer, and where those tracks had to cross highways, the place at which they did so was regarded as a crossroads as if they were two highways crossing each other. Speeds were low on mineral lines and there was never any question of grade separation by the building of bridges. Nor was there any great change when main line railways began to be built, especially in the eastern side of England away from hilly areas.

Level crossings quickly became commonplace all over the country when the building of railways on a large scale began in the 1830s, and it was not long before the interface between road and rail on the same level was recognised as a potential source of danger. Trains drawn by steam-driven locomotives created a much greater danger than horse-drawn rakes of wagons, and travelled much faster. They took longer to stop. It was clear that some form of regulation was necessary in the interests of safety.

The early railways

The building of a railway created the need for it to cross roads and tracks that lay in its path. Each new railway company had to employ surveyors to determine the route of the railway, which then formed the basis of a parliamentary Bill seeking authority to build the line. Parliamentary powers were necessary in order to be able to obtain the land on which the railway was to be built. The Bill would specify the arrangements to be provided by the railway company at each level crossing, which might include providing a crossing keeper on a private road to accommodate objections to the Bill by a local landowner.

Below: A nostalgic view of the past. A Midland-type signalbox controls this very long skew-crossing at Wisbech North, on the Midland & Great Northern Railway. In this photograph, taken on 4 October 1958, the train departing (behind Class 4 2-6-0 No 43109) is the 11.11am from Peterborough North to Yarmouth Beach. Two more signalboxes can be seen in the next few hundred yards. The M&GN closed later that year. *Frank Church*

Level Crossings

Right: Weaverthorpe signalbox is a rather unusual structure and controls a gated crossing on the York–Scarborough line of the former York & North Midland Railway, dating back to 1845. This photograph dates from 1970. *F. W. Smith collection*

Below: Many stations on the Southern had a level crossing near the end of the platform. This gated crossing is controlled by Robertsbridge 'B' signalbox, but since this photograph was taken, on 5 September 1969, the gates have been replaced by manually-controlled barriers. *J. Scrace*

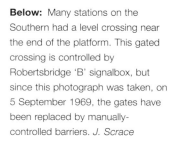

In the early days of railways, where roads and footpaths had to be crossed, it was usual to do so at the same level, creating a level crossing, although in some cases a bridge would be proposed or required, especially where topography simplified the construction of a bridge either under or over the railway. As the 19th century progressed and industries developed, towns grew and road traffic increased. Many more roads were built and level crossings became an increasing impediment to the smooth flow of road traffic. As a result, the highway authorities became increasingly reluctant to accept more level crossings.

The beginning of general regulation regarding level crossings

By the late 1830s it was evident that some general rules were needed regarding level crossings, both for safety purposes and to achieve standardisation throughout the country, allowing the process of debating railway bills to be accelerated. The railway companies considered this to be desirable for commercial reasons; Parliament did so to speed up the expansion of the railway network, and brought in the Highway (Railway Crossings) Act 1839. The actual wording of the Act stated (Section 1):

Above: The gated crossing at Burton Station South signalbox, closed many years ago, must have caused problems when opened for road traffic. Burton-upon-Trent had a very complex system of private railways operated by the brewery companies, connecting with the main-line railway companies that served them. This photograph dates from 1957. *F. W. Smith collection*

'Wherever a railroad crosses or shall hereafter cross any turnpike road or any highway or statute labour road for carts or carriages in Great Britain, the proprietors or directors of the said railroad shall make and maintain good and sufficient gates across each end of such turnpike or other road as aforesaid at each of the said crossings, and shall employ good and proper persons to open and shut such gates, so that the persons, carts or carriages passing along such turnpike or highway shall not be exposed to any danger or damage by the passing of any carriages or engines along the said railroad ....' (The Act applied to all then existing and to subsequent railways.)

Thus the use of gates and gatekeepers became, at an early date in railway development, an important legal requirement at public level crossings and a very significant development which lasted virtually unchanged for over a century until automatic half-barrier level crossings were introduced under the British Transport Commission's Act of 1957. The use of the term 'railroad' instead of the more general term 'railway' is noteworthy, illustrating the view that a railway was merely just another form of roadway, but with rails on it.

The 1839 Act gave rise to the question of the relative priority of road and rail traffic at a level crossing. Many of the earlier private Acts (known as Special Acts) had provided for the gates to be normally across the railway line, but more and more this was found to be unsatisfactory. Road traffic could stop easily if the gates were

closed across the road, but the same did not apply to trains, which were becoming faster, heavier and more frequent. Level crossings were increasingly places of danger and of delay to trains.

The situation was remedied by the Railway Regulation Act 1842, which in Section 9 stipulated that level crossing gates were to be kept constantly across a public road when not required to be opened for road traffic (unless the Board of Trade were to order otherwise). The 1842 Act also gave the Board of Trade powers in Section 13 to authorise companies to construct bridges in place of level crossings at their own expense, although it should be noted that it did not give the Board powers to compel them so to do.

The terminology of highways

Before proceeding any further, it would be useful to explain the various terminologies applied to highways etc, in the early Acts referring to level crossings.

'Highway' is a generic term, meaning a way over which members of the public have the right to pass and repass. It is often referred to as the King's (or Queen's) Highway. It includes roads used by wheeled vehicles (then carts and carriages), bridleways and

Right: The very unusual signalbox at Knaresborough, pictured in 1949, is built on to the end of a row of houses. The level-crossing gates are worked by hand.
F. W. Smith collection

Below: The attractive signalbox at Lymington Town, photographed in 1972. Remotely-controlled barriers have since replaced the gates, and the crossing is now monitored by CCTV. *J. Scrace*

footpaths. It should be noted that the right is to pass and repass only, although a pause for refreshment is allowed.

A public road is a highway provided for the passage of carts and carriages (and now motor vehicles).

A turnpike road was a road built by trustees on which tolls were charged for its use. Trusts were formed by businessmen, merchants and local people wishing to improve the passage of wheeled vehicles between main centres, but such schemes had to be authorised by private Acts of Parliament because powers were needed to acquire the necessary land. The new railways merely followed the same procedure. By 1838 there were 22,000 miles of turnpike road, which incidentally is almost the same mileage of railways that existed at their peak in 1913. Highway Boards were established under the Highways Act 1835 and gradually replaced

the turnpike trusts. The last turnpike ceased to operate in 1895, but many of the toll-houses remain to this day and are easily recognisable.

Private level crossings

There are two types of private level crossing:

Occupation Crossings

These were provided where the line of route of the railway crossed an existing private road, usually a dead-ended road leading from a highway to a farm or a group of buildings, or even a hamlet. The requirements regarding construction and use were (and still are) radically different from those concerning public level crossings. The user of the private road is responsible for the safe use of the crossing, including both his own safety and the safety of trains. Field gates are provided which open away from and do not close off the railway, which is the opposite to the arrangement at most public level crossings. The user is legally required to 'shut and fasten' the gates after use, with a penalty for failure to do so. It should be noted that there may be public footpath rights over a private level crossing, but it would be unusual to find separate wicket gates for pedestrians next to the road gates. Anyone with a valid reason for visiting the property to which an occupation crossing gives access has a legal right to use the crossing. This extends much wider than the owner or occupier of the property, and includes friends who are visiting, tradesmen and the postman.

Accommodation Crossings

When a railway was built, it frequently happened that the line of route crossed a piece of land in single ownership, which would thus be divided into two separate areas. Access was often required between the two areas of land, and level crossings were provided

to enable such access. Many still remain, but some have fallen into disuse. Legal and constructional requirements are identical to those covering occupation crossings.

The requirement to fence

The Special Acts for the construction of a railway contained many provisions, including those concerning fences, and Section 10 of the 1842 Railway Regulation Act stipulated that all railway companies must erect, maintain and repair sufficient fences along their respective lines. These provisions were consolidated in the 1845 Railways Clauses Act, requiring a railway company to make and at all times thereafter maintain 'Sufficient posts, rails, hedges, ditches, mounds or other fences for separating the land taken for the use of the railway from the adjoining lands not taken, and protecting such lands from trespass, or the cattle of the owners or occupiers thereof from straying thereout, by reason of the railway…..' (Section 68). Thus was imposed upon the railway companies a legal and burdensome duty to fence both sides of the line throughout its length, but it was only for the convenience of the owners or occupiers of land adjoining the railway. It had nothing to do with the safety of the public and was not intended to prevent them from straying on to the railway. Rather, it was to stop those on the railway from trespassing on private land.

That same Act also tightened up crossing construction by requiring, for instance, the provision of 'convenient ascents and descents' for road traffic (Section 61). This was to prove of some significance many years later.

Below: Coxbench was on the Little Eaton branch, connected with the Derby–Chesterfield main line of the erstwhile Midland Railway at Little Eaton Junction. It was not a block post, and the signals, here still showing their Midland parentage, were worked by the station porter, who also controlled the gates. *F. W. Smith collection*

Above: These gates at Uffington are operated manually by the signalman and, owing to their length, overlap when open to the road. The station was closed about 50 years ago, but the architecture of the stationmaster's house, pictured in 2007, continues to recall the Midland Railway line between Stamford and Peterborough, opened in the late 1840s. *Stanley Hall*

More legislation

During this period of railway development, questions concerning level crossings continued to receive considerable attention, indeed much more so than the normal operation of the railways. The provisions of the Act of 1839 were repeated in an 1845 Act, the cumbrously named Railways' Clauses Consolidation Act (often referred to as the Railways' Clauses Act) which brought together the provisions of several separate and often private Acts authorising the making of railways, and was intended to simplify the progress of Railway Bills through Parliament. Level crossings were only one of many subjects which the Act dealt with in its 165 Sections.

Section 46 stated that: 'If the line of the railway cross any turnpike road or public highway, then … either such road shall be carried over the railway, or the railway shall be carried over such road, by means of a bridge …' There is an exception to this requirement where the Special Act providing for the building of the railway specified a level crossing.

Section 47 amplified the provisions of the 1839 and 1842 Acts referred to earlier, by stating that the gates should be so constructed as to fence in the railway when closed. It also stated that the normal position of the gates was to be across the road, but the Board of Trade could order the normal position of the gates to be across the railway 'if they are satisfied that it will be more conducive to the public safety …'. The concern for public safety is interesting, as it would be just as safe whichever was the normal position of the gates. It has become the normal practice to consider the volume and nature of road traffic and the impracticality of closing the gates across the road if there is a heavy flow of road traffic. The Railway Rule Books do not normally intrude into the realm of the law, but the old Rule 118 (later Rule 99) stated that: 'Unless special authority be given to the contrary, the gates at level crossings must be kept closed across the roadway, except when required to be opened to allow the line to be crossed.'

There is an interesting enactment in Section 48 that imposed a speed limit of four miles an hour on all trains when crossing a turnpike road on the level adjoining (to) a station. This was not confined to trains which actually stopped at that station.

As the 19th century progressed, with the concurrent growth of road and rail traffic, level crossings continued to be matters of concern. In 1855 a House of Commons Standing Order imposed a new duty on the Railway Inspectorate (of the Board of Trade) to report upon level crossings proposed in Railway Bills. The House of Commons felt that bridges were preferred to level crossings if they were not too costly, but that they should be provided as a matter of course over or under important roads unless there was very special difficulty in doing so. Thirty-five people unconnected with railways were killed at level crossings in that year.

There was a further Railways Clauses Act in 1863, which had an interesting provision in Section 5, stating that '… it shall not be lawful for the company in shunting trains to pass any train over the level crossing, or at any time to allow any train, engine, carriage or truck, to stand across the same'. The need for such an enactment would seem to indicate that delays to road traffic at level crossings were already becoming a nuisance.

There were two other important provisions in the 1863 Act. Section 6 stated that: 'For the greater convenience and security of the public, the (railway) company shall erect and permanently maintain a lodge at the point where the railway crosses on the level the turnpike road or public carriage road …' It also required the appointment of 'a proper person to watch or superintend the level crossing'. In practice, this requirement would only apply where the level crossing was not at a signalbox where the signalman operated the gates.

Gatekeepers had already been required under the 1839 Act and no doubt some form of shelter would have been provided for them. Presumably they also satisfied the description of 'proper persons'. There are no records of two separate people being employed.

Section 7 stated that: 'The Board of Trade may, if it appears to them necessary for the public safety, … require the company … to carry the turnpike road or public carriage road either under or over the railway by means of a bridge or arch, instead of crossing the same on the level …' Note that the requirement refers to the safety of the public, not their convenience in the reduction of delay. Curiously, but possibly wisely, the drafter of the Act also felt that it was necessary to state specifically that the provision of a bridge exempted the railway company from the requirements regarding lodges and attendance. It would appear that even then vexatious litigants were not unknown.

The significance of the 1863 Act is plain to see. Railways authorised after that date contain few level crossings.

Public footpaths and bridleways

These are regarded as highways, but the only requirement imposed upon the railway companies was given in Section 61 of the 1845 Act, which stated that, in relation to level crossings, '… the company shall at their own expense make and at all times maintain convenient approaches, with handrails and other fences …'. For a footpath there should be 'good and sufficient' gates or stiles. For a bridleway, gates only were required. There is no reference to the safety of the crossing users and for many years they were expected to look out for their own safety. If the view of approaching trains was limited by the curvature of the line, a 'Whistle' board might be erected.

A footpath is defined as a highway 'over which the public have a right of way on foot only'.

A bridleway is defined as a highway 'over which the public have a right of way on foot and a right of way on horseback or leading a horse'.

The establishment of a Railway Inspectorate

It was one thing to lay down constructional and operating requirements, but it was necessary to see that they were adhered to. The rapidly developing railway system in the 1830s soon attracted parliamentary attention, and it was felt that some control over the railways was necessary in the public interest. A Parliamentary Select Committee was therefore appointed in 1839 to consider the question and its recommendations led to the Regulation of Railways Act of 1840. This short Act came into force on 10 August 1840 and commenced 'Whereas it is expedient for the Safety of the Public to provide for the due Supervision of Railways …'

Among its relevant provisions were 'No railway may be opened for the public conveyance of goods or passengers without a month's notice being given' (Section 1) and 'The Board of Trade may appoint persons to inspect railways' (Section 5).

The Inspectors were drawn from the Corps of Royal Engineers, as being men with the necessary knowledge and experience, and likely to be impartial. They had no powers other than inspection and could not prevent an unsafe railway from being opened. This careless loophole was closed in the 1842 Regulation of Railways Act, which gave the Board of Trade power to postpone the opening of a new line if an Inspector reported that the opening 'would be attended with danger to the public using the same' (Section 56). The same Act also made provision for safety at level crossings regarding the position of the gates (Section 59), which was incorporated in the 1845 Railways' Clauses Act.

To summarise

During the period up to 1863, many important principles were laid down concerning level crossings, which continued in operation for the next century. Some are still in force. But the construction of new railways was continuing at a tremendous pace and Parliament felt it essential to lay down some standards regarding their construction and operation. In 1850 there were 6,621 route miles of railway open for traffic. By 1860 the mileage had reached 10,433.

The significant and enduring requirements concerned the provision of a lodge at all public-road level crossings and a 'fit and proper' person to operate the gates. Two types of public-road level crossing emerged. As the century progressed, it became commonplace to erect a signalbox, especially if the level crossing were adjacent to a station. The signalbox would then act as the lodge and the signalman would be the 'fit and proper' person to operate the gates. In between stations, crossing keepers were appointed to operate the gates and they were provided with a cottage next to the crossing in which to live. In the 1850s there would probably be little road traffic, so although the hours were long the work would be light.

The legal requirement to fence the line was noteworthy, and set Britain apart from railway systems abroad. Initially it was done for the convenience of the adjoining landowner, but as time went by it was extended by common law to members of the public, especially where children were concerned.

Left: Heslerton signalbox, on the York–Scarborough line, was located not far from that at Weaverthorpe (pictured on page 6) and followed the same architectural style. Class 31/1 No 31 246 passes with the 11.10 Scarborough–Sheffield on 9 August 1980. The York–Scarborough line runs across fairly flat agricultural land and, owing partly to its relatively early construction, has many level crossings; between Malton and Seamer — a distance of 18 miles — there are 34, most of them being private crossings, mainly of occupation status. The remainder, save that at Weaverthorpe, have now been equipped with automatic half barriers, which have replaced the signalbox and gates seen here. *Keith Smith*

2

CONSOLIDATION, 1863-1914

Signalling, Operation and Safety of Level Crossings

At signalboxes

By the 1860s, signalboxes had become an integral part of the train signalling system but were not normally provided solely to control level crossings, although where practicable a signalbox would be located next to one, so that the signalman could superintend the working of the crossing (a legal requirement) and operate the gates. Significantly, road traffic passing over a crossing was not considered to constitute an obstruction to trains. The Train Signalling Regulations required the line to be clear before a signalman could allow a train to approach his signalbox from the signalbox in rear, but the signalman could allow a train to approach even when the gates were across the railway and whilst road traffic was passing over the level crossing. Level crossings were protected by the normal lineside Stop signals so far as train movements were concerned.

The signals were interlocked with the level-crossing gates, so that they could not be cleared for a train to pass unless the gates were across the road. The interlocking was achieved mechanically. Similarly, once the signals had been cleared, the gates could not be moved from the 'Closed across the road' position. The interlocking would prevent it.

The signalman would determine the moment at which he should put his gates across the road in order to avoid delaying the train. The signals had to be cleared for a train before the Distant signal came into the driver's view and this could result in the crossing being closed to road traffic for several minutes, depending on the speed of the approaching train.

In almost all cases, there would be a railway Stop signal a few yards on the approach side of the level crossing, and a train could be allowed to run up to that signal at Danger even though the gates were still across the railway. The driver would have been warned of

Below: This undated photograph of Hunmanby crossing and signalbox shows the timeless architecture of signalboxes, level-crossing gates and wicket gates and, corporate signing aside, could have been taken at almost any time in a period of 100 years. All would be swept away and replaced by automatic half barriers. Hunmanby lies near the Yorkshire coast between Bridlington and Filey, on a line that is riddled with level crossings. Between Driffield and Filey, a distance of 25 miles, there are 13 automatic half-barrier crossings, 13 private crossings, 2 CCTV crossings, a manned barrier crossing and a miniature-warning-light crossing. *D. Ibbotson / F. W. Smith collection*

this by the Distant signal being at Caution. In some track layouts there would have been an additional Stop signal some distance on the approach side of the level crossing, and the Signalling Regulations would have required the signalman to keep that signal at Danger until the approaching train had been brought quite or nearly to a stand, thus providing an additional warning.

In some cases the gates were operated by a wheel in the signalbox, but at quieter signalboxes, when there was time for the signalman to leave the signalbox, the gates would be swung across by hand. It is obvious that the signalman had to pick an opportunity to

Above: A semi-rural scene near Pitsea station, on the Tilbury loop, on 24 May 1959. This appears to be a user-worked crossing with pedestrian wicket gates, and the line is in the process of being electrified. It is now a full-barrier crossing, remotely controlled, and monitored by CCTV. *Frank Church*

close the crossing to road vehicles and this could be a matter of some nicety when there was a heavy flow. Warning lights had not been invented, and the only indication that the road user had of the imminent closure of the gates was when they actually started to

Left: Coalville crossing, on the Leicester–Burton line, with single gates worked from the adjacent Midland-style signalbox. Today there are lifting barriers controlled remotely from the nearby Mantle Lane signalbox, and the crossing is monitored by CCTV.
M. A. King / F. W. Smith collection

13

Level Crossings

move, very slowly at first if road traffic was heavy. Signalmen became expert at the procedure, but it was an unsatisfactory situation even in the days of horse-drawn traffic. When motor vehicles came into use the situation could become quite difficult.

Smaller swing gates, known as wicket gates, were generally provided for the benefit of pedestrians wishing to cross and in many cases could be mechanically locked by the signalman to prevent access when a train was approaching. The signalman was allowed to leave the gates unlocked for a period after he had closed the main gates across the road, and he would use his judgement as to when he should lock them. The Rule Book merely stated that '… the Signalman must operate the controlling arrangement (i.e. the mechanical lock) whenever it is necessary to prevent persons from crossing the line' (Rule 117). It was usually possible for the signalman to lock each gate individually to give some flexibility when deciding when to lock them. Footbridges were provided at some locations to allow pedestrians to cross the line even when the level-crossing gates were across the road.

There were some crossing boxes which looked like signalboxes and controlled signals which protected the crossing, but they did not regulate the passage of trains.

At public road crossings not controlled from signalboxes

There were several hundred of these and there were many variations between different railway companies in their signalling and operation. In the simplest cases there were no railway signals, and the crossing keeper had to telephone the signalman to ask for permission for the crossing to be used. In some cases the block signalling instruments used by signalmen, and which showed whether a train was approaching the signalbox or not, were duplicated at the level crossing for the guidance of the crossing keeper. Before the days of telephones and block instruments the crossing keeper had to rely upon the timetables and listen for the sound of an approaching train. 'Whistle' boards would be erected in some cases.

Left: Makeshift crossing arrangements with the daily Wadebridge–Wenford Bridge freight trip at Dunmere Siding, on the Southern Region of BR. The locomotive is a Beattie 2-4-0 well tank, No 30587. The guard is holding up a red flag to warn motorists that a train movement is imminent. The date unknown, but it's all history now. *J. C. Haydon*

The gates at these crossings were often of the field gate type, opening away from the railway, and were normally kept closed across the road. When a vehicle needed to cross, the far gate would be opened first, to avoid its having to stop on the crossing.

The provision of railway signals varied from location to location, and from railway company to railway company. In some cases, only a Distant signal was provided, a large red disc on the crossing gate acting as a Stop signal. Occasionally a full set of signals would be provided. In many cases, especially at quiet crossings, the signals would be kept in the Clear position, which was not a fail-safe situation. Accidents happened when the Distant signal was placed at Caution after the train driver had passed it in the Caution position. It was not a satisfactory situation, but the companies were not prepared to invest in better signalling arrangements, and it has to be said that the situation existed until comparatively recently. It was one of the main reasons in the 1960s for the installation of automatic half barriers and other forms of equipment not requiring attendance. The early railway companies seemed satisfied with a philosophy that a big steam engine at the front of a train could easily push a horse-drawn vehicle on a crossing out of the way.

The Rule Book gave some guidance to the crossing keeper. Rule 119 stated that 'When it is necessary for the Line to be crossed … the Gatekeeper must, before opening the gates, satisfy himself that no train is near; he must then place his Fixed Signals (where provided) at Danger to stop all coming trains, and such signals must remain at Danger until the Line is clear, when he must close the Gates across the roadway, and then take off [i.e. clear] the Signals.' The rule gives no guidance as to how the gatekeeper should satisfy himself that no train was near. Presumably it was left to his common sense, an unusual procedure, but no doubt the rule-writer felt that it was too difficult to spell it out in detail: the situations would vary from one crossing to another.

However, whilst the big steam engine/small cart philosophy might hold good in most cases, there were exceptions when heavier and larger vehicles and farm machines began to be used. The writer of Rule 120 had a field day:

'Traction, or other heavy engines, heavy loads of timber, &c, or droves of animals, must not be allowed to cross the railway when any train can be seen, or is known to be, approaching in either direction.

'Station Masters must personally request users of Traction and other Road engines in their neighbourhood to give notice to the nearest Station-master on each occasion of their intention to pass such engines over the railway, either at an Occupation Level Crossing or at a Public Level Crossing not provided with fixed signals. (The word "fixed" means signals on a post which is fixed in the ground).

'On receipt of this intimation the Station-master must arrange for a man, with hand and detonating signals, to be sent out at least three-quarters of a mile from the level crossing in each direction to secure the safety of trains during the passage of the traction or other engines across the railway. If the staff at the station will not admit of a man being sent in each direction, the services of platelayers must be obtained.'

If the crossing was used without the proper notice being given, the Station Master had to report the matter to his superior.

Above: Hensall signalbox lies on the former Lancashire & Yorkshire Railway between Knottingley and Goole. North Eastern Region influence is apparent in the provision of boom gates, which are still in use. This photograph was taken on 8 June 2006. *F. W. Smith*

At quiet crossings, the cottage might be occupied by a track worker, whose wife would operate the gates during his absence at work, thus providing an additional income.

At private level crossings

Throughout the 19th century the legal position of private level crossings, either of the occupation or accommodation type, remained unchanged. The railway companies' obligations ceased once they had provided the necessary approaches, the field gates and the surface over the railway, other than to maintain them. The user was required to look out for his own safety and to close the gates after crossing, with a penalty for failure to do so. The most that a railway company might do was to provide 'Whistle' boards. Courts held that the duty of an engine-driver was to observe the railway signals and the track, and he had no duty towards road users by specially looking out and sounding the whistle, although he would be expected to whistle if he happened to see a road user about to cross. The whistle would be sounded not in the interests of the safety of the road user, but in the interests of the safety of the train. It has to be said that crossing the line in fog, at a private crossing, could be a hazardous business.

At bridleway and footpath crossings

The railway companies' obligations were explained in the previous chapter, being to provide a suitable way to and from the crossing and to provide pedestrian or bridle gates, or stiles. It was up to users to look out for themselves. It was often the practice to provide 'Beware of Trains' boards or 'Stop, Look and Listen' boards, often then made of cast iron, whose durability is evident to-day. There would also usually be a Trespass notice, quoting the legal authority and the penalty for non-observance.

Towards the end of the 19th century, Parliament became seriously concerned about the number of people killed whilst crossing the line at level crossings, and the Railway Inspectorate produced a report showing that in the five years 1888-92, 369 people had died, as follows:

On public carriage roads	141
On private or occupation roads	98
On footpaths	106
On footpath and occupation roads combined	24

In its report to the House of Lords, the Inspectorate detailed the proposals which the railway companies had in mind for dealing with the problem, which included the building of a large number of footbridges and a number of other bridges. Under the Railways Clauses Act of 1863 the Board of Trade could subsequently require a railway company to erect, at its own cost, a bridge in place of a level crossing, if this appeared necessary for public safety (Section 7).

By way of comparison, in 2006 only six pedestrians (excluding trespassers) were killed at level crossings, as follows:

At an automatic open crossing locally monitored 2
At an occupation crossing with a telephone 1
At an occupation crossing 1
At a footpath crossing 2

However, in the same year, 242 people were killed who were classified as trespassers and suicides, of whom only one was aged under 16.

The replacement of level crossings by bridges

Until about the 1840s, Britain was mainly an agricultural country, and large towns and centres of population were few. Trains were infrequent and ran at low speeds. The delays to horse-drawn vehicles at public-road level crossings were not a serious inconvenience.

However, as the century progressed, Britain rapidly became a highly industrialised country, whilst at the same time trains became more frequent and ran at higher speeds. Delays to road traffic reached unacceptable levels in major centres and the replacement of level crossings by bridges became more frequent, with the powers contained in the 1863 Railways Clauses Act being invoked. Actually, the justification for replacement was often on the grounds of public safety, rather than convenience. However, when the Board of Trade required the London & North Western Railway to replace the busy level crossing across its main line at Atherstone (Watling Street, now the A5) by a bridge the LNWR procrastinated. The company had to be compelled to do so through an injunction obtained by Warwickshire County Council, which included the imposition of a 4mph speed limit on trains passing over the level crossing. Ironically, this would have the effect of the level crossing being closed to road traffic for a longer period than if trains had been allowed to pass over at normal speed.

Readers will have noticed many places where bridges have replaced level crossings. They will also have noticed that the earlier railways had many level crossings and not many bridges, whilst this situation was increasingly reversed as the century progressed. One of the best examples was Hull before the layout was rationalised in the 1960s. The former North Eastern Railway, beginning in the 1830s, had an extensive network in the city and docks of Hull with many level crossings, but the Hull & Barnsley Railway, which was not authorised until 1880, was mainly built on an embankment with roads passing under, avoiding that need. The Hull & Selby Railway, authorised in 1836, still has many level crossings, as does the York–Scarborough line, built in the 1840s.

Later on, larger railway companies were probably quite glad to build lines without level crossings. The cost would be included in the whole outlay of the line, and would be a small proportion of the total, whilst there would be no permanent costs for the staffing and maintenance of level crossings.

A position of stability is reached

By the 1870s, the railway scene with its white-painted, heavy wooden gates across public road level crossings became familiar throughout the land. Sometimes there were wicket gates for pedestrians. It was a scene that would be as familiar in the middle of the 20th century as it would have been generations earlier, except that the queues of traffic would then consist of motor vehicles (and cyclists in some areas) instead of fine shire horses

Below: Pictured in June 1972, this crossing at Rylstone lies on the Skipton–Grassington branch, now cut short at the major quarry complex a mile further along. The gates are worked by the traincrews.
D. Ibbotson / F. W. Smith collection

drawing carts, and even finer horses pulling the carriages of wealthier people. It was an astonishing example of stability.

The public at large would not be familiar with private level crossings, but they would be used to footpath and bridleway crossings, although unaware of the distinction. They would be accustomed to looking out for their own safety, although a 'Whistle' board might be erected on the approach to the crossing if the view of approaching trains were restricted.

A new threat appears
The year of 1896 was significant in the history of road transport in Britain. The Daimler Motor Co of Coventry built its first motor car and a host of small-scale motor car businesses were founded, some of which became household names including Humber in 1896, Riley in 1898, Standard in 1903 and Rover in 1904. The Vauxhall Co built its first car in Britain in 1903, and in 1905 the Austin Motor Co was formed in Longbridge, Birmingham. Motoring was still only for the wealthy members of the middle and leisured classes, but in 1908 annual production topped 100,000 for the first time, some of which was exported.

Above: This fine former North Eastern Railway signalbox at Starbeck South, between Harrogate and Knaresborough, controls the gated crossing. The gates seen in this photograph, taken on 29 August 1972, have since been replaced by manually-controlled barriers. *M. A. King / F. W. Smith collection*

By 1914 there were 132,015 licensed private cars on Britain's roads.

So far as level crossings were concerned, motor cars travelled faster than horse-drawn vehicles and covered greater distances. They passed over many level crossings, and had the potential to cause accidents, especially at private level crossings, but whilst the occupants of cars may have impaled themselves on level crossing gates, there is no record of railway passengers having lost their lives following collisions between cars and trains during this period.

Nonetheless the emergence of the motorised road vehicle significantly altered the road/rail relationship at level crossings. This was not in any legal sense, but because a motorised road vehicle was potentially a greater threat to rail safety than a horse-drawn vehicle.

THE RISE OF MOTORISED ROAD TRANSPORT, 1919-39

3

Railway level-crossing gates were designed to fence off the railway when they were closed across the road, and they were strong enough to deal with most situations. However, the development of the motor car created a new hazard and there was worse to come.

The motor lorry appears

The motor lorry appeared very rapidly as a consequence of wartime demands for the motorised transport of *matériel*. When the war ended, in 1918, the Government's need for those vehicles ceased, and they were offered for sale to members of the public, being snapped up quickly by ex-servicemen, especially those who had been trained in the army as lorry drivers or mechanics, and paid for by their gratuities on demobilisation. The road haulage industry was formed and grew quickly.

In the inter-war period, the number of licensed road vehicles grew rapidly, year by year.

	1920	1930	1939
Private cars/light goods	187	1,056	2,034
Heavy goods	101	349	488
Motor cycles	288	712	418
Buses, coaches, taxis	75	101	90
Other	–	54	118
Total	**651**	**2,272**	**3,148**

All figures are in thousands.
(*Source: Transport Statistics Great Britain, Department of Transport*)

Below: Lincoln has long been plagued by its level crossings. Here Class V2 2-6-2 No 60803 heads over the crossing at the east end of the station and on to the GN/GE Joint line with the daily Newcastle–Colchester service on 15 June 1956. *R. E. Vincent*

The effect on public level crossings was relatively small. There were occasional collisions with the gates, but there were very few accidents in which railway passengers were killed. The only change which the railways needed to make concerned the normal position of the gates. By law, the normal position was across the road, and that could only be changed by the Ministry of Transport, which would place an order on the railway company concerned exempting the company from the requirement to normally have

Above: Ex-Southern Railway Class Q1 0-6-0 No 33005 takes a train of empty stock over the gated level crossing at Appledore and heads towards Ashford on 21 February 1961. Automatic half barriers have now been installed at this location. *M. Edwards*

Right: The view south over the level crossing at Morar, a few miles south of Mallaig, in August 1968. The gates were worked by hand at that time, but the crossing has since been converted to an automatic open crossing locally monitored (AOCL). The train driver approaches the crossing at such a speed as will enable him to stop if he sees that the crossing is obstructed and he also checks a repeater light that shows whether the road traffic signals are flashing. *C. Lofthus*

Left: A sylvan scene long since vanished. A newly-introduced diesel railcar stands in Long Melford station with a train from Colchester to Cambridge via Haverhill on 14 June 1958. The route on the right led to Bury St Edmunds. This part of East Anglia suffered severely in the so-called Beeching closures. Note the foot crossing for the use of the station staff.
G. R. Mortimer

the gates closed across the road, and requiring the normal position of the gates to be across the railway, except when a train needed to pass. That exemption was given to many level crossings.

The main effect of the greater number of motor lorries in use was felt at private level crossings of the 'occupation' type, and examples of some of the more serious accidents will be given later in this chapter.

The expansion of the road network and the replacement of level crossings by bridges

The increase in road traffic had two effects on level crossings:.

The expansion of the road network

Britain's road network had developed slowly and was designed for horse-drawn, short-distance traffic. Motorised road traffic needed better roads. By-passes of major towns were needed to relieve the pressure of traffic in town centres, and new trunk roads were needed to provide for long-distance road haulage. Where these new roads crossed railway lines, bridges were built and no new level crossings were required.

The replacement of level crossings by bridges

This had started in the decades before World War 1 and the process continued in the years between the two wars. There are many examples to be seen up and down the country, one of the best known being the imposing bridge over the East Coast main line at Crescent Junction, just south of the station at Peterborough.

Accidents at public level crossings

During the period 1922-5, the annual average number of fatalities at public level crossings was 12. There was far more concern and public irritation at the delays to road traffic caused by level crossings. Within the city boundaries of Hull there were no fewer than 13 level crossings, five of which were on tramway routes.

Here are some examples of the more serious level-crossing accidents:

Collision at Fenny Stratford, LMSR, 7 December 1925

In terms of fatalities, this was one of the worst level-crossing disasters on record. At 8.34pm on 7 December 1925, the 6.30pm local train from Cambridge to Bletchley was slowing down for the station stop at Fenny Stratford when a motor vehicle crashed through the public-level crossing wooden gates and was hit by the train. The motor vehicle was a two-year-old, one-ton Ford which had been adapted to carry passengers in charabanc-type transverse seats. This vehicle had run away on the down gradient approaching the level crossing owing to the driver's error of judgement in failing to control his speed properly. It had 14 seats, and they were all occupied by a private hire party, plus the driver.

Although the motor vehicle was travelling at only 10mph or so when it crashed through the level-crossing gate, and although the train was travelling at only about 10-12mph as it slowed down to stop in the station, the motor vehicle was wrecked. Six of its passengers were killed outright and a further three died in hospital, including the vehicle driver. Four more passengers received serious injuries and only one member of the party escaped uninjured.

The level crossing had four wooden gates, controlled by wheel from the adjacent signalbox, and they were interlocked with the signals. The train was hauled by a former LNWR 2-4-0 of the renowned 'Jumbo' class, No 1170, and consisted of three coaches and a brake van. The leading bogie of the second coach was derailed, but there were no injuries to passengers or traincrew.

Collision at Naworth, LNER 30 August 1926

Naworth was a small wayside station on the line between Newcastle and Carlisle, 10 miles west of Haltwhistle. Only a few trains called there and the normal daily traffic averaged 15 passengers and eight milk cans. There was a level crossing at the station which carried a minor public road from the main A69 road; it had field gates instead of the normal gates, and the normal (legal) position of the gates was across the road. There was no signalbox at the crossing and the signalboxes on each side were

Right: The site of Naworth station; this was the view east towards Haltwhistle on 30 July 2007. The former stationmaster's house is being renovated and automatic half barriers have replaced the old gates. The photograph gives some idea of the limited view the train driver and the charabanc passengers would have had of each other on that disastrous day in 1926. *Stanley Hall*

Low Row and Brampton. The block instruments in the signalboxes for this section had repeater indicators at Naworth so that the porter there could tell when a train was expected.

Distant and Stop signals were provided in each direction, and these were normally in the 'Off' (Clear) position. They had to be replaced to the Caution and Stop position respectively when the crossing gates had to be opened to allow road vehicles to cross the line, but the signals were not interlocked with the gates. These were free to be moved at any time.

Road traffic was light, but on this day a charabanc approached the crossing. It was a typical open passenger vehicle, with five transverse seats and a collapsible hood, and was well-loaded with passengers enjoying a day out. The engine of the vehicle was rated at 26hp.

The porter had worked at Naworth for only a week, having been made redundant at Edlingham, on the Alnwick–Coldstream line. He saw the charabanc approach and opened the gates for it to cross before it had actually stopped, and it began to cross at walking pace. At this moment a passenger train came into view, only a short distance away owing to curvature of the line. The charabanc driver saw it and tried to accelerate but he was unable to avoid a collision. The eight-coach passenger train, the 1.18pm express from Newcastle to Carlisle, headed by a 4-4-0, No 1029, was travelling at about 50mph and its driver did not see the charabanc until he was very close, far too late to reduce the speed of his train. In the ensuing collision the charabanc was wrecked and eight of the passengers were killed. Three were seriously injured. It was 2.38pm.

Right: The heavily-wooded setting of the crossing at Naworth, recorded on 30 July 2007. *Stanley Hall*

Left: The Newcastle–Carlisle line was one of the very early railway lines to be built, dating from 1838, hence its many level crossings. No one thought of building bridges in those days. Around the village of Denton, between Haltwhistle and Carlisle, there are no fewer than six crossings in a mile – two automatic half-barrier crossings, three private crossings and one manned crossing with gates. The latter, at Denton Village, is used only infrequently, and a small sign on the gate states 'Ring for Crossing'. This photograph was taken on 30 July 2007. *Stanley Hall*

The porter was also killed. He had omitted to look at his block instrument repeaters, which would have told him that a train had already passed the last signalbox, Low Row, only a mile away from the crossing. He had also failed to put his signals back to Caution and Stop, but in the event it would have been too late to avoid the collision. The train would already have passed the Distant signal. It transpired that the signals were quite often not put back when the gates were opened to allow a road vehicle to cross.

This crossing was reasonably well provided with safeguards, if the working instructions were carried out by the porter. Lt-Col Mount, who held a public inquiry into this accident, recommended that normal public level-crossing gates should be installed, and that they should be interlocked with the lineside railway signals. This would ensure that the signals would be put back to Caution and Stop before the gates were opened to allow road traffic to cross. However, it would still be necessary for the porter to check his block instrument repeater indicators to remind him not to put his signals back if a train had already passed the last signalbox on the approach to the crossing. This would avoid the danger of the signals being put back after the engine driver had passed the Distant signal.

Accidents at occupation crossings

Collision at Shepreth occupation crossing, 17 August 1928

The 10.0am express from Cambridge to King's Cross had hardly got into its stride when, at 10.11am, it ran into a motor lorry

Left: Another relic of the past, at Lane Head, a mile from Denton. This gated crossing sees very little use other than by the local farmer, but staffing it requires four non-resident crossing keepers, working shifts. It has stop signals interlocked with the gates, and repeater block indicators to show when it is safe to put the signals back to danger and open the gates to allow users of the crossing to pass. *Stanley Hall*

Right: Ivatt Class 4 2-6-0 No 43008 climbs through Woodend, on the line from Sellafield to Moor Row, and over the gated crossing on 21 September 1967. The line is now closed. *D. H. Wilson*

Below: The elegant new footbridge that was brought into use in 1954 at Bathgate Lower (ex-LNER), on the line between Edinburgh Waverley and Glasgow Queen Street Low Level via Airdrie, to allow passengers and others to cross the line when the wicket gates were locked for a train. The line from Edinburgh currently terminates at Bathgate, but the Scottish Assembly has plans to re-open it. *BR*

crossing the line at the occupation crossing. The locomotive, Atlantic No 3253, was derailed but ran on for about 100yd before sheering off to its left and being completely turned round by the weight of the following train. The fireman was killed and the driver was injured. Five of the six coaches were derailed, but only one passenger was taken to hospital.

The lorry was a 6-ton 45hp Dennis loaded with lime, and its driver was killed. He had failed to ensure that no train was approaching before moving over the crossing. Col E. C. Trench, one of the Railway Inspecting Officers, held a public inquiry into the accident and commented particularly on the problem of the growth of heavy road transport.

Collision at North Belton Farm occupation crossing, *14 May 1929*

Col Trench's comments were echoed the following year, when the lorry involved in this accident, an unladen 4/5-ton four-wheeled Leyland flat wagon, was one of a fleet of 50 lorries owned by Messrs Alexander Smart of Leith. The lorry driver failed to exercise proper caution before moving onto the line, and was killed. The crossing lay on the East Coast main line between Dunbar and East Linton, and the train concerned was the down 'Flying Scotsman', hauled by a Pacific locomotive, No 2746 *Fairway*. It was not derailed.

Collision at Wharf Road occupation crossing, 27 November 1934

In fog, the 8.31 am express from Cambridge to London Liverpool Street collided at 50mph with a 2-ton unladen Chevrolet lorry, between Broxbourne and Cheshunt. Unfortunately the rear axle of the lorry became tangled under the locomotive and derailed one pair of the bogie wheels. The locomotive, 4-4-0 No 8896, ran on until it hit a crossover and fell over onto its side, killing the driver and fireman. One coach was badly damaged and two of the coaches fell over onto their sides. One passenger and the lorry driver were taken to hospital. The train carried 110 passengers. The lorry driver was held responsible for the accident.

Concerns regarding safety at private level crossings

The frequency of collisions and casualties is shown in the following table, giving average annual figures:

	1924-9	1930-4	1935-8
Number of collisions with no casualties	18	18	27
Number of collisions with casualties	19	22	28
Number of derailments	1.5	1.5	1.5
Number of occupants of road vehicles killed	6	4	5
Number of passengers and railway staff killed	0.2	0	1
Number of pedestrians killed	7	7	10

It is interesting to note that the expected increase in collisions in the period 1935-8 did not result in any rise in the number of derailments and only a slight increase in the number of fatalities.

On 29 October 1938, an express train crashed into a lorry at Third Willow Row Drove, between March and Ely, in thick fog.

Above: Hand-operated gates, with protecting signals, just south of Criccieth. Photographed on 22 September 1988, they would be replaced a week later by an automatic barrier crossing locally monitored (ABCL). *Mike Wore*

The engine driver and fireman, and the lorry driver, were all injured. East Anglia probably has more level crossings, both public and private, than any other part of the country and certainly more accidents, mainly due to the amount of agricultural traffic using occupation crossings.

A question was raised in the House of Commons early in 1939 about the safety of private-road level crossings, and the Minister of Transport, in his reply, gave some interesting detail:

Accommodation crossings and their purpose in 1939 (includes all private crossings)

Access from field to field	18,615
Access from farm or private estate to public road	2,809
Access to industrial land, used by heavy vehicles	437
Access to camping grounds, sports grounds	85
Effectively public crossings through usage	224
Miscellaneous	486
Total	**22,656**

These would have varied extensively in the amount of usage; some like the industrial land at relatively frequent tervals, while access to sports grounds suggests only occasional use but quite heavy when in operation. A different source stated that there were also more than 4,000 level crossings of railways over public roads.

Right and below: Manually-operated tubular steel road gates and wicket gates at Llanfair PG, a mile towards Holyhead from the Britannia Bridge over the Menai Strait, pictured on 24 May 2007. A rather faded sign at the signalbox gives the full name of the village, with a convenient English translation. *Stanley Hall*

A correspondent in the April 1939 *Railway Magazine* had also voiced his concerns about the dangers of occupation crossings. He had witnessed a heavily-loaded haywain being taken across an important main line which carried a frequent service of express passenger trains. The cart was hauled by a pair of horses and he asked one of the carters how they knew if a train were coming, and the reply was simply "Oh, we 'as a look". They did not seem to appreciate the danger, as the visibility in neither direction was more than 500yd, about 15 seconds' travelling time for an express train travelling at 60mph. The procedure for crossing was to open both gates, draw the cart forward into the gateway, after which one of the men would step into the six-foot and look up and down the line. If he saw or heard nothing he would call out to the other man, who would whip up the horses and cross. The correspondent commented that in those days of elaborate signalling precautions, such a procedure as the one he had witnessed seemed to be lacking in the first elements of safety. And, it might be added that the situation improved only slowly until well after World War 2.

Collision at Cross Drove occupation crossing, 1 June 1939

This crossing, adjacent to Hilgay station, on the LNER between Downham Market and Ely, was the site of a collision on 1 June 1939 between a passenger train and a lorry passing over the occupation crossing (from which a clear view of straight railway track was possible for a considerable distance in each direction). All five coaches and the engine and tender were derailed, and there were four fatalities.

The train was the 11.2am passenger service from Hunstanton to Ely, hauled by 4-4-0 No 8783 (incidentally one of the two Royal Train engines) and was travelling at 60-65mph. The lorry was a 2-ton Ford laden with straw.

There was some confusion on the lorry regarding the opening of the gates. The driver's mate went across to open the far gate and the driver took this as an indication that it was safe to cross. The train was close by, but the driver's mate, who could clearly see in the fine clear weather the train approaching at speed, took no steps to stop the lorry driver. The lorry was wrecked, but one of its wheels became lodged under the engine's bogie, derailing it. The engine ran forward until it struck a diamond crossing and became fully derailed, together with three of the following coaches, which scraped along a number of wagons standing in the siding alongside, suffering severe damage. Three passengers were killed outright and one died in hospital in the worst private level crossing accident of the inter-war years. Five were seriously injured.

The lorry driver was tried for manslaughter and dangerous driving at Norfolk Assizes on 11 October 1939, but was found not guilty.

Modernisation

The railway companies would have been glad to adopt the modernisation of public level crossings, as had been done in Europe and North America, provided a good financial case could be made and provided the Ministry of Transport could be persuaded to agree to such a policy. There would have been two benefits. For the railways, the prize was the automating and unstaffing of level crossings. For the Ministry, the prize was the reduction in delays to road transport in waiting for trains to pass which automatic crossings could provide.

However, in the 1930s, the railway companies never had adequate funds for all desirable investment, and the modernisation of level crossings was well down the list. But in view of the potential benefits to road users, the Ministry could have taken the initiative and provided funds. However, the reality was that any funds available had to be devoted to improving existing roads by widening and straightening, and by the building of by-passes and a limited number of new roads. They were the priorities. The end result was that low priority was given to the development of automatic crossings by both the railway companies and the Ministry. The general economic situation both at home and abroad in the 1930s did not help the case. And the railway companies saw no reason why they should help their road haulage competitors by reducing delays at level crossings.

THE POSTWAR YEARS, 1945-67

Change comes slowly

4

The postwar situation for the railways

The railways ended the war with heavy arrears of maintenance. In addition, there was much that they wanted to do to modernise the system and to improve safety. They had optimistically assumed that the considerable surplus funds which had accrued during the war would now be available for those purposes, but they had reckoned without the duplicity of governments. The surplus funds never reached the railways, and in any event the return of a Labour Government in 1945 ensured that the railways would be taken into public ownership.

At the end of the war level crossings, with a few exceptions, had been unchanged for many years. Their heavy wooden gates, operated from an adjacent signalbox or crossing box, or pushed across by hand, closed the road for several minutes, with significant disruption to road traffic but several factors ensured that postwar plans did not include level-crossing improvements. Modernisation of the signalling, and the introduction of automatic train control to minimise signals passed at danger, were higher on the agenda. Damaged or destroyed stations and goods depots had to be dealt with. And on top of everything else there was a shortage of staff, and particularly of technical staff.

Below: An early example of lifting barriers and warning lights at Warthill signalbox, on the line between York and Hull, closed since this photograph was taken in 1952. The 'Stop' banner was pivoted. *BR*

Above: Britain's first automatic half-barrier crossing with flashing red road-traffic signals was brought into use on 5 February 1961 at Spath, on the now-closed line between Uttoxeter and Ashbourne. An electrically-illuminated sign displayed a 'Second Train Coming' message. *BR*

Right: It became the practice to distribute explanatory leaflets to people in the area, describing in some detail the working of the crossing. It included the admonition 'Wait — don't zig-zag', recognising even in those early days this potential hazard to trains (and reckless car drivers). *BR*

The first fully automatic level crossing barriers in this country...

LOOK INSIDE FOR FULL DETAILS

1953 — a typical year

The number of level crossings in Britain in 1953 was as follows:

Public-road crossings with gates	4,256
Public-road crossings without gates	249
Occupation and accommodation crossings	21,311

The number of people killed at level crossings was as follows:

Gatekeeper at a public crossing	1

Occupants of road vehicles

At public crossings with gates	3
At public crossings without gates	1
At occupation and accommodation crossings	15

Pedestrians

At public crossings with gates	8
At occupation and accommodation crossings	10
At footpath crossings	7

Some of the more serious accidents

At Ystrad Caron occupation level crossing on 5 May 1953 in broad daylight a train travelling at only 25mph struck and demolished a motor van which was passing over the crossing, killing all six occupants. The crossing, which served four farms and some playing fields, had the usual field gates and there was good visibility along the line. The van driver was found to be solely to blame and it was stressed that the safety of both trains and road vehicles depended entirely on the care taken by the drivers of road vehicles. In practice this private crossing had also acquired a certain amount of public use, which always tended to be a problem as will be seen in other accidents.

At the little-used Moulinearn public level crossing, near Pitlochry, on 8 September 1953 a freight train travelling at moderate speed in daylight ran into and wrecked a tractor and trailer, killing both occupants. The gates were kept locked across the road and the gatekeeper was required to get permission from the signalman at Ballinluig before opening them. He had failed to do so. Errors by gatekeepers were one of the reasons for introducing automatic half barriers (see below), because they eliminated human error on the part of railway staff. Unfortunately, they transferred the responsibility for safety at automatic crossings to the drivers of road vehicles, all of whom were also prone to human error, and some of whom behaved less responsibly than railwaymen.

The Modernisation Plan 1955

The Modernisation Plan, entitled the Modernisation and Re-equipment of British Railways, envisaged spending about £1,200 million for a thorough modernisation of the railway system, its traction and its trains. Steam was to be eliminated and the Government backed the plan. There was no mention of level crossings. The new nationalised railways saw little purpose in spending money on modernising level crossings for other people's benefit. But the omission had not gone unnoticed in high places.

Left: A similar AHB installation was brought into use on 3 June 1962 at Little London crossing, Stallingborough, on the line to Grimsby and Cleethorpes. *BR*

Below: A large explanatory notice board was erected at the roadside at Little London crossing. Some changes were later made to the operating sequence and the crossing equipment. *BR*

A significant breakthrough in the modernisation of level crossings

Level-crossing modernisation and automation had been proceeding apace on some Continental railways for several years. France led the way with 700 automatic half-barrier installations by 1956, whilst Belgium and Holland had hundreds of open crossings with automatic flashing lights only. Britain had almost none.

At the same time there was growing concern both within the British Transport Commission and the Ministry of Transport about the cost of manning thousands of level crossings, and the delays to the increasing volume of road traffic when the gates were closed to road traffic several minutes before a train arrived there. Moreover, national prosperity and full employment were making it difficult to obtain reliable men for the simple but responsible safety duties at level crossings. Level crossings worked by signalmen were very safe, but those crossings worked by crossing keepers were less so, because in many cases their equipment had not kept pace with improvements in technology.

There had been growing awareness of the developments in France and the Low Countries, and when, in June 1956, the Chief Inspecting Officer of Railways, Lt-Col G. R. S. Wilson, happened to meet the heads of their railway administrations, he took the opportunity to request that a party of officers from Britain should visit their systems to study their methods of protecting level crossings. It was a fortuitous meeting that was to have far-reaching consequences. The request was readily granted and the visit took place in October that year.

The party consisted of two Inspecting Officers and two road engineers from the Ministry of Transport, and two officers from the BTC (a signal engineer and an operator). They visited 46 level crossings in the three countries in 10 days and came away with a firm conviction that some of the Continental methods of operating level crossings would prove suitable for adoption in Great Britain without prejudice to safety. It was a major step forward. The report of the visiting party was signed on 14 March 1957.

Specifically, their report said that the automatic half-barrier equipment which had been developed in recent years on the Ccontinent had undoubtedly been successful, and should prove to be safe in Britain. The French system provided for five seconds of flashing red road-traffic signals followed by the fall of the automatic half barriers, which had to be horizontal five seconds before the arrival at the crossing of the fastest train. The Dutch system provided a few seconds longer, but in both countries the time between 'strike-in' and arrival of the fastest train at the crossing was between 20 and 25 seconds.

The proposed adoption of automatic half barriers (AHBs) in Britain was a quite dramatic change. Continental road users had become accustomed to automatic level crossings for many years, and there were differences in the legal framework and in road user behaviour. The reaction of Britain's road users was an unknown factor. The barriers would not be interlocked with railway signals and they would not close off the crossing. The crossing would be unsupervised. The old bogey of the danger of trapping something

Right: In the early 1960s full-width lifting barriers without flashing red lights were installed at Oxmardyke level crossing, between Selby and Hull, and were operated from the adjoining gatebox. *BR*

between unmonitored gates would disappear, because the half barrier would be on the approach side of the crossing by road and there would be no barrier on the exit side of the crossing. However, the adoption of AHBs would presuppose that no road vehicle would stall on the crossing and that no road vehicle would be held up on the crossing when in a queue of traffic which had come to a stand for any reason. Road engineering might ameliorate the latter, but it was still an act of faith and it took some years before the method of operation of AHBs became common knowledge among road vehicle drivers.

The early years would test the validity of those assumptions. It emerged that the British public had an instinctive distrust of unstaffed, automatically-operated level crossings and referred to them scathingly as 'Continental crossings' as though they were somehow immoral. The fact is that the British public loved their gated crossings. They could understand gates and knew how they worked. They would need to be educated in how automatic half-barrier crossings worked and how safe they were if used properly. This was done in practice every time a new crossing was introduced, by the distribution of explanatory leaflets, especially to schools, and by local meetings. Holding such a meeting could be

quite an experience and required particular skills, but it was found that children accepted AHBs much more readily than their parents.

The plain substitution of lifting barriers for gates at attended level crossings had already been legalised by the BTC's Private Act of 1954, subject to approval in each case, but it did not permit the removal of attendants. Trials were carried out at Warthill (on the now-closed line between York and Hull via Pocklington) with the lifting barriers worked from an adjacent signalbox and interlocked with the railway signals. New legislation would be required for AHBs, but the BTC was looking ahead and had already included a clause in Section 66 of its annual Bill for 1957 to legalise AHBs. This clause enabled the Minister to authorise 'barriers…..and automatic and other devices'.

Hasten slowly

It was generally accepted that such a fundamental change in level-crossing protection should be undertaken gradually, and in any case time was needed to design this entirely new piece of equipment, including the flashing road-traffic signals and the general road configuration. Highway engineers of the Ministry needed to be closely involved in such matters as minimum road width, the design of the road-traffic signals, the limits of vertical curvature to prevent the grounding of long, low road vehicles, road markings and road traffic signs. This was a new venture for them.

In 1958, 51 people were killed at level crossings, as follows:

	Public road crossings		Occupation/ accommodation	Footpaths	Totals
	with gates	*without gates*			
Railway passengers	2	–	–	–	2
Railway staff	6	–	–	–	6
Road vehicle occupants	5	6	21	–	32
Pedestrians	8	1	–	2	11
Totals	**21**	**7**	**21**	**2**	**51**

Automatic half-barrier crossings would do nothing to tackle the growing problem of danger arising at occupation and accommodation level crossings, caused by industrial and agricultural changes. These changes often resulted in increased road-traffic levels, with heavier lorries and farming machinery creating a serious risk to the lightweight diesel multiple-units now coming into use, especially on secondary lines where such private crossings were more common.

One such private crossing was Funtham's Lane, which crosses the Peterborough–March line at an occupation crossing serving two brickfields (The London Brick Co and Fletton's). The site had developed extensively over the years, leading to the increasing use of the crossing by heavy lorries, although an accident on 27 April 1958 concerned a car which was crossing the line and was struck by a passenger train running from March to Peterborough. The car was wrecked and three occupants were killed. The level- crossing gates were open when the car

Left: Funtham's Lane level crossing, seen here on 27 September 2007, has all the appearance of a public road but is in fact an occupation crossing which at one time served a busy brickworks and became notorious for accidents, which virtually compelled BR to install full barriers interlocked with the railway signals, operated and monitored from the nearby King's Dyke signalbox. *Stanley Hall*

Left: King's Dyke signalbox, between Peterborough and Whittlesea, has manually-controlled barriers, as seen here on 27 September 2007. The signaller also operates and monitors Funtham's Lane crossing, half a mile away. *Stanley Hall*

Right: Moulinearn level crossing, a few miles south of Pitlochry on the former Highland line, was the site of an accident in 1953, as described in the text. In those days the road was a public right of way, and the gates were worked by a crossing keeper who lived in the house alongside. The crossing now has private status and has electrically-operated barriers and miniature warning lights, as seen in this photograph, taken on 10 October 2001. *Stanley Hall*

Below: Hillam Gates signalbox controls a level crossing just south of Milford, on a section of the York–Church Fenton–Pontefract route. Photographed on 13 March 1962, these manually-controlled barriers, without flashing red road-traffic signals, are now controlled remotely and monitored by CCTV. *BR*

approached the crossing, although the instructions state that they should be closed after each vehicle. However, the volume of traffic had rendered this almost impossible to enforce in practice. The daily use was 500 motor vehicles (mainly lorries), and 400 motor cycles or cycles.

Funtham's Lane must have ranked as one of the most accident-prone private crossings in the country, as there had been previous accidents in 1930, 1932, 1936 (when a lorry driver was killed), 1947 and 1957. After the 1936 accident, indicators were provided on both sides of the crossing, showing either 'Line Clear' or 'Train Coming – Stop'. There were also instruction notices. It also transpired that the 'Train Coming' sign, which was automatically illuminated by an approaching train, was often showing for several minutes before the train arrived, leading to regular disobedience.

It was eventually replaced by lifting barriers operated from the nearby King's Dyke signalbox and monitored by CCTV. And it ought to be noted that the wrecked car was removed from the line, and the train went forward to Peterborough, only 55 minutes after the accident.

The other type of crossing about which there were concerns for safety, and which it was hoped could be replaced by automatic half barriers, was the crossing worked by a gatekeeper, and not by a signalman in the controlling signalbox. The dangers at such locations were well illustrated by an accident at Roundstone level crossing near Angmering, on the Brighton to Portsmouth line, at 9.31am on 22 September 1965.

In thick fog, a four-coach electric multiple-unit smashed through the level-crossing gates which had been wrongly replaced across the line after the train had passed the Distant signal for the crossing in the clear position. The train ran into a double-decker bus which soon caught fire and was quickly burnt out. Three of the bus passengers were killed and eight were injured. There were no injuries on the train.

Both lines were blocked by the bus, but the wreckage was quickly cleared and the line was reopened six hours after the crash. Those were the days when it was considered essential to reopen the line after an accident as quickly as possible in order to minimise the inconvenience and delay to passengers.

Right: General view of Berwick
signalbox and level crossing,
between Eastbourne and Lewes,
as seen on 5 September 1968.
J. Scrace

Right: General view of Berwick
signalbox and level crossing,
between Eastbourne and Lewes,
as seen on 5 September 1968.
J. Scrace

The level crossing was provided with Distant and Stop signals in both directions, and the crossing keeper was made aware of the need to place the gates across the road by repeater block indicators and block bells. He saw a queue of traffic waiting to cross, with the bus at its head, and he became confused and replaced his signals to Danger and immediately put the gates across the railway to allow road traffic to cross. All would have been well had he waited a minute or two after putting his signals back to Danger before putting the gates across the railway. By that time the train driver, who would have already passed the Distant signal at all clear, would have come upon the Stop signal at Danger whilst travelling at normal speed and would have passed over the crossing with the gates still across the road, eventually coming to a stand several hundred yards beyond the crossing. There would have been no danger to either road or rail traffic.

This was typical of many accidents at such crossings, and Col Reed, who held a public inquiry into the accident, said that automatic half barriers would provide a safer alternative. He hoped that the road layout could be so designed to enable automatic half barriers to be installed there. These were the early days of AHB installations.

Right: Pedestrians and cyclists
move forward as the barriers
begin to rise at Lancing
manually-controlled barrier level
crossing, Southern Region.
Ian Allan Library

A milestone — Britain's first automatic half-barrier (AHB) level crossing

On 5 February 1961, an event took place at the small village of Spath which was the precursor of level crossing modernisation in Britain. Many thought it was long overdue. Spath lies on the now-closed line between Uttoxeter and Rocester, and the road is the B5030 between the same two points. It was equipped with half barriers, twin red, alternately flashing, road-traffic signals, and a sign which became illuminated when a train was approaching from the opposite direction.

For some years, the Railway Inspectorate took a very cautious stance, and initially AHB crossings were allowed only where the daily motor traffic did not exceed 1,000 vehicles and where the maximum speed of trains did not exceed 60mph. These requirements were more restrictive than those in operation on the continent of Europe; therefore in 1963 another study tour of officers from the Ministry and the British Railways Board (BRB) was made to France and Holland. It was found that France now had over 1,300 AHB crossings, with over 4,000 crossings suitable for conversion. They were all in rural areas. The Dutch already had 200 installations, many at busy sites, and were introducing new ones at the rate of one a week.

On the return of the party to Britain, the Ministry eased its former cautious approach. In 1966 it issued a revision of its Requirements, allowing AHBs to be installed in rural areas where road traffic did not exceed 150 per hour in each direction, with no restriction on train speeds. In built-up areas there was no limit on the volume of road traffic, provided it could readily clear the crossing (depending mainly on road layout). The danger of road vehicles being trapped on a crossing when their forward progress was impeded for any reason was fully appreciated. At automatic crossings the entire responsibility for preventing collisions between trains and road vehicles, and for the safety of trains, was thrown upon the road user. It was a very significant change and represented a major shift in the philosophy of railway safety.

The installation of AHBs rapidly accelerated, as shown below (number of crossings in use at the year-end):

1964	15
1965	56
1966	124
1967	205

There were 1,500 more in the pipeline, and there were plans to install about 150 crossings per year.

By the end of 1967, there were 2,425 public level crossings on British Railways, made up as follows:

Crossings with signal protection

Operated from a signalbox	954
Operated by a gatekeeper, with interlocked signals	453

Crossings not protected by signals

Operated by a gatekeeper, with no interlocked signals	516
Automatic crossings	205
Other crossings	297

The method of operation of automatic half-barrier crossings in 1967

The descent of the barriers was initiated by an approaching train at a point 24 seconds' running time from the crossing at the maximum permitted speed of trains. The process was triggered by the front wheel of the train striking a treadle at the initiation (or strike-in) point, together with the occupation of a track circuit (an electrical train detection device). The red road-traffic signals then began to flash alternately for eight seconds, after which the barriers descended in a maximum of eight seconds. There was

Left: Unusually the gates at St James Deeping signalbox, on the line from Peterborough to Spalding, swing away from the line when the crossing is open for road traffic to pass. The signalbox structure is very well maintained, as apparent from this view, recorded on 27 September 2007.
Stanley Hall

then a further period of eight seconds before the fastest train could arrive at the crossing. The lights continued to flash until the barriers rose, which they did as soon as the rear of the train had passed over the crossing, actuated by another treadle. This brisk operation was important in order to deter impatient motor vehicle drivers from zigzagging round the barriers. It was important to understand that the operation of the barriers was not in any way connected with the normal signalling of trains, and the railway signals were not interlocked in any way with the operation of the crossing. There is separate provision for slow trains where the time-increase to reach the crossing is more than 40 seconds.

The different presentation of the road-traffic signals to the road vehicle driver at a railway level crossing, compared with the red/amber/green presentation at a normal road junction, is quite deliberate. At a road junction the lights change frequently, and if the same system were to be applied at a railway level crossing the green aspect could be displayed for extended periods of time, with the risk that the road user might not observe any change in the aspect. Flashing lights are also considered to be more visually arresting.

The operation of the barriers for a single train is therefore quite simple and quick. The next question is: how is a second train to be dealt with when it is approaching the crossing? In the 1966 Requirements, if a second train 'strikes in' before the first train has passed over the crossing (i.e. before it has 'struck out') the barriers will remain down and the road traffic signals will continue to flash. If, however, the second train strikes in whilst the barriers are rising after the previous train has struck out, the barriers will continue to rise and when they have become vertical, the road traffic signals will flash and the bells ring for only six seconds, followed by the normal eight-second descent, and a shortened period of about five seconds before the second train reaches the crossing. It might be thought that such a rapid re-flashing sequence for the second train, and the quicker arrival of the train at the crossing, might unnerve a road vehicle driver unused to such an occurrence and cause him to panic and stall his engine on the crossing. It was important for road vehicle drivers to understand that after being stopped at the crossing they should not begin to move forward until the barriers had become fully raised, so that they could remain stationary when the lights began to flash again and the bells start to ring.

The operation of the crossing equipment is monitored from a signalbox, and a telephone is now provided at the crossing connected directly to that signalbox. Various road signs are provided on the road approach to the crossing.

The safety record of automatic half-barrier crossings up to the end of 1967

The first accident at an automatic half-barrier crossing occurred at Cleghorn, between Carstairs and Motherwell, on 11 December 1965, when a car driver became confused and stalled his car on the crossing. There were three other accidents all caused by drivers zigzagging round the lowered barriers.

There was a similar 'stalled car' accident at Trent Road Crossing, Beckingham, near Gainsborough on 16 April 1968 which, whilst outside the time scale of this chapter, is relevant because the circumstances at the crossing were based on the 1966 Requirements. A driver and five passengers in an Austin A40 saloon car had stopped at the crossing when the red road-traffic signals began to flash. When the barriers rose, the car moved forward, and the lights began to flash again for a train in the other direction. The car driver stalled his engine and owing to a defective starter motor was unable to restart it. He scrambled out of the car and attempted to push it off the crossing but within a matter of seconds the car was swept away, killing the driver and its five passengers. It was time to reconsider the 'second train coming' sequence.

Accidents and fatalities at level crossings in 1967

The number of level crossings of various types was as follows:

Manned with gates or barriers	2,047
Unmanned with automatic half barriers	198
Other unmanned public level crossings	177

Fatalities at level crossings of various types were as follows:

Manned with gates or barriers	
Railway staff	0
Occupants of road vehicles	2
Pedestrians	5
Automatic half barriers	1
Occupation and accommodation crossings	
Occupants of road vehicles	2
Pedestrians	6
Footpath crossings	
Pedestrians	2
Total fatalities	**18**

Compared with 10 years earlier, the number of public level crossings had almost exactly halved as a result of the line closures under the 1963 Reshaping proposals (known as the Beeching closures). The number of occupation crossings had more than halved. These reductions tended to reflect the rural nature of many lines that were closed, on which level crossings were more common. Many occupation crossings were little used, and some of those of the accommodation type (i.e. field to field) had fallen into disuse. However, so far as automatic half-barrier installations were concerned, the future looked secure, but events were to prove otherwise. Hardly had 1968 dawned when the installation of new AHBs was to come to an abrupt halt, with only a handful being dealt with in the next 10 years. They were truly the wasted years. Why? This will be revealed in the next chapter.

DISASTER STRIKES

5

The year 1968 opened on a note of optimism. The programme for the installation of automatic half barriers was in full swing and there were hundreds more in the pipeline. The twin fears of accidents caused by vehicles stalling on the crossing and road traffic blocking back across the crossing had proved almost (although not quite) unfounded, and no one envisaged the ultimate horror of a huge load travelling so slowly that it could not pass over the crossing in the minimum time of 24 seconds and might therefore provide a massive obstacle to a train. But just in case, a notice at AHB crossings read 'IN EMERGENCY or before crossing with exceptional or heavy loads or cattle PHONE SIGNALMAN'. Surely nothing could be clearer than that?

The ultimate horror occurs

A 120-ton electrical transformer had to be moved by road seven miles from the English Electric Co's works at Stafford to its depot on a disused airfield, which lay just beyond an automatic half-barrier level crossing at Hixon. Hixon lies on the electrified main line from London Euston to Manchester Piccadilly via Stoke-on-Trent. The automatic half barriers had been installed in April 1967.

The movement of the transformer was entrusted to the heavy haulage firm of Robert Wynn & Sons Ltd. It used a specially strengthened 32-wheel trailer, powered and guided by a six-wheel traction unit at each end, the whole assemblage being 148ft long, and 16ft 9in at its highest point. The journey was authorised by a special order issued by the Ministry of Transport, which set out the route to be taken, and the journey was escorted by two police constables in a police patrol car. It took place on 6 January 1968.

The police car led the way over the level crossing and the transporter followed about 60yd behind, travelling at a speed of about 4mph. When it reached the crossing, its driver reduced speed to 2mph, so that three members of the transporter crew could walk alongside to check the clearances between the top of the transformer and the overhead electric wires, and between the lowest

Below: Eight miles after passing over Hixon level crossing and three months after the disaster there, a London-bound express headed by an 'AL6' (Class 86) electric locomotive approaches Meaford level crossing at Stone on 28 April 1968. The traditional gates at this location have since been replaced by full barriers, remotely controlled and monitored by CCTV. *K. P. Lawrence*

Right: The original pre-Hixon design of automatic half-barrier equipment, as installed at Stallingborough by the Eastern Region in 1962. The most obvious feature is the absence of an amber light under the twin flashing lights. Note also another reminder of times gone by — the long row of telegraph poles, which accompanied the traveller on almost every train journey. *BR*

Below: The post-Hixon design of traffic signals and warning signs, with the new amber light and the new, so-called secret sign, illuminated only when required. This was a very expensive piece of equipment, which helped to make conversion to an automatic half-barrier crossing unaffordable. *T. G. Flinders*

part of the trailer and the ground. At 2mph, a distance of 148ft would take almost 50 seconds to pass any specific point, and there was a possibility that the movement would have to be halted if any clearance were found to be inadequate either above or below the transporter. It was possible to adjust the trailer a few inches either up or down. When the leading traction unit was driven onto the crossing, its driver knew that it would take at least a minute to clear the crossing, provided no adjustment needed to be made, which could take a few minutes. It seems quite clear that the idea that a train might approach at any time never entered anyone's head.

The leading traction unit had crossed the two railway lines, and the transporter was straddling them, when a 12-coach London-bound express train travelling at about 75mph 'struck-in' about 1,000yd away. It was less than half a minute from the crossing and, with the train driver's view of the transporter on the crossing restricted to 400yd, there was no time to reduce the speed of the train. Disaster was inevitable. The driver of the leading traction unit had already passed the road-traffic signals at the crossing before they started to flash, but he saw the train approach and attempted to accelerate. That very slight acceleration managed to move the transformer from the direct path of the train, so that the impact took place only a few feet from the end of the transformer, shearing the connection between the centre part of the transporter and its rear bogie and hurling the transformer to the left of the line, thus fortuitously reducing the scale of the disaster. Nevertheless, eight passengers and three members of the train crew were killed and 45 were injured. The train continued its forward progress for about 100yd before coming to a stand, the electric locomotive being derailed along with several coaches, some of which were badly damaged.

The inquiry into the cause of the accident

For almost a century, every inquiry into a railway accident, including the most serious ones such as Harrow (1952), Lewisham (1957) and Hither Green (1967), had been conducted by one of the Inspecting Officers under the powers of the Regulation of Railways Act 1871, but the same Act also made provision for inquiries of a judicial nature, and the Minister of Transport chose the latter route owing to the number of non-railway organisations involved. The Inspecting Officers of the Railway Inspectorate had been fully involved in the development of the new level crossing standards and had overseen the way those standards had been applied to Hixon Crossing. They had also given the necessary statutory approval to changes in the crossing. Therefore, the Inspectorate quite properly thought that it would have been difficult for an Inspecting Officer to hold the inquiry because it could be said that he would have been investigating the decisions of the Inspectorate.

Mr Edward Brian Gibbens QC was therefore appointed to hold an investigation into the circumstances of the accident and to inquire generally into the safety of automatic half-barrier installations and make recommendations. He famously commented that 'In the presence of modern technology the old gates are a creaking anachronism.'

The hearings were held over 41 days, and 63 witnesses gave evidence on oath. The parties involved in the accident were the English Electric Co, which required the transformer to be transported; the Ministry of Transport, which provided the special order setting out the route; the Heavy Haulage Co, which was hired to carry the transformer; the Police, who escorted the journey; and British Railways. The evidence presented at the inquiry by each party is now examined.

Above: No doubt here as to what the drivers of abnormal loads should do. The post-Hixon alterations required the introduction of the 'Park Here and Use Phone at Crossing' arrangements, together with a telephone and lay-by at each side of the crossing — another expensive change. The location is Black Dyke AHB crossing, near Arnside, the date 10 July 2007. *Stanley Hall*

Below: Class 26 diesel No 26 034, running light, approaches the gated level crossing at Longforgan on its way from Perth to Dundee in September 1986. The gates have been replaced by manually-controlled barriers. *Stanley Hall*

The English Electric Co

Mr J. H. Preston was the company's Chief of Heavy Transport at Stafford. He said that he knew the Hixon crossing well and passed over it almost once a week, but he had never seen it in action, nor did he know about its 'brisk operation'. Before the accident on 6 January six other abnormal loads had passed over the automatic crossing, but on that morning Mr Groves, the transporter driver, requested directions from Mr Preston, who merely mentioned the level crossing at Hixon as a landmark and did not warn him that it was an automatic crossing, nor that there were overhead electric wires. He made no mention of the Emergency Notice regarding the need to telephone the signalman before crossing, which he must surely have seen during his numerous journeys over the crossing. An opportunity to save the day was lost.

The Ministry of Transport

The Ministry issued a 'Special Route Order' stipulating, among other things, the route to be followed, the haulier to give six days' notice to all highway and bridge authorities, and chief officers of police. Note that there was no mention of automatic level crossings. However, before laying down a route, the Ministry consulted all highway and bridge authorities, chief officers of police and divisional road engineers. It was the firmly held view of the Ministry that the information was to be taken in the nature of advice, and it was unnecessary to issue cautions in respect of hazards which were visible and capable of being appreciated by the driver of the vehicle. Unfortunately, the driver of the heavy haulage vehicle did not appreciate the hazard at Hixon level crossing.

As a result, it had not been the practice to include level crossings, and it had not really been necessary to do so before the introduction of automatic crossings with their brisk operation altered the situation. And unfortunately it had not been British Railways' practice to inform the Special Route Order section of the Ministry of the installation of any automatic crossing; nor was such information transmitted to them by the Railway Inspectorate. Two opportunities to prevent the Hixon accident were missed.

Robert Wynn & Sons Ltd

The crew of the transporter did not know the time sequence of operation of automatic crossings, and so they did not realise they would have insufficient time to cross safely. Nor had any of them observed the Emergency Notice requiring them to telephone the signalman before crossing. The haulage firm had not ensured that its drivers knew about automatic crossings and the vital need to telephone the signalman. Had it done so, the accident would not have happened.

When the transporter reached Station Road, Hixon, one of the escorting police officers told the driver, Mr Groves, that there was a 16ft 6in headroom sign ahead, and a level crossing with a slight hump. Mr Groves already knew that there was a level crossing at Hixon because he had been told about it by the English Electric Co before he left Stafford. Mr Groves then saw the level-crossing warning sign and realised he was approaching an automatic level crossing, but said that he did not think that the barriers could be

Left and below left: Two views of the High Street gated crossing at Lincoln. In the first, recorded in April 1973, Class 31 diesel No 5577 passes with train 1D19, the 13.56 Great Yarmouth–Doncaster, while on 24 May 1980 a sister locomotive heads the 12.20 (SO) Skegness–Leeds.
Robert C Reding; Brian Morrison

set in motion whilst he was on the crossing. He did not see the headroom sign, but fortunately he had been warned about it by the escorting police.

Groves proceeded onto the crossing in the full knowledge that he might be straddling it for some time if the transporter had to be lowered to clear the overhead wires, or if it had to be raised to avoid grounding. Indeed, it might have grounded during the lowering sequence and become immobilised. To drive on to the crossing faced with such a scenario might be considered folly of a high order, but none of the crew members had received any

instructions from their employer about the special hazard at automatic half-barrier crossings.

Initially the haulage firm asserted that they did not know how automatic crossings worked and had no idea of the 'brisk' operation, but that was not so. One of their drivers had been involved in a near miss at Leominster AHB on 8 November 1966 and the firm wrote to British Railways about it. The somewhat acerbic reply from BR addressed to one of their directors, Mr H. P. Wynn, left the firm in no doubt about the timing sequence at AHBs. The firm eventually admitted at the inquiry that they

Right: Class 40 diesel No 40 179 heads south through St Bees, on the Cumbrian Coast line, with a train of empty soda-ash hoppers from Workington to Northwich on 28 July 1982. The level crossing here has since had its gates replaced by manually-controlled barriers operated from the signalbox. *Brian Dobbs*

Below: The 10.37 DMU from Boston to Nottingham passes over the gated level crossing at Rauceby on 15 July 1979. This line and its gated crossing still survive, and the signalman still has to swing the gates by hand, but the DMU is no more. *John C. Baker*

ought to have recognised, but did not do so, the need to advise all their employees about the nature of automatic level crossings and the vital need to telephone the signalman. However, the consequences of one of their vehicles grounding or stalling on an automatic crossing did not occur to the firm, nor that the time needed to cross with an abnormal load might exceed the time available to do so before a train reached the crossing. The penny did not drop.

However, Robert Wynn & Sons *was* clearly aware that there was an extremely short time for any heavy vehicle to traverse an automatic crossing. The letter from BR made it perfectly clear. But they failed to reach the blindingly obvious conclusion. As the report says, in this state of ignorance, and the failure to draw the glaring inferences from the events which had taken place in their

own business, the management failed to give any instructions or warning to any of their drivers as to the hazards of automatic crossings. Robert Wynn and Sons Ltd bore a heavy (but not the entire) responsibility for this accident.

The police

The police knew about the load on 29 December 1967, when Wynn's sent them a copy of the special notice relating to the journey, but they were not notified until the morning of the journey, when Police Headquarters received a telephone call that the load was ready to leave Stafford. Neither of the two escorting policemen was in any way prepared for the duty of escorting the load, and neither of them had ever been to Hixon. Both had been posted to motor patrol duties in the Stone Division only five days

Left: A Class 205 DEMU forming the 15.45 Ashford–Hastings approaches Ferry Road gated crossing shortly after leaving Rye station on 21 September 1978. This crossing is now equipped with remotely-controlled barriers and CCTV. *G. Wright*

before. One might have expected them to have been given time to reconnoitre the route beforehand to familiarise themselves with anything unusual en route, such as the automatic level crossing at Hixon. They might even have noticed the instruction regarding telephoning the signalman before crossing, so yet another opportunity to avoid the accident was lost.

During the journey, the escorting police told Mr Groves, the transporter driver, about the hump on the level crossing as well as the headroom restriction. It was not strictly part of their duties, which were really confined to regulating road traffic to allow the passage of the abnormal load. Mr Groves thought that they had wider responsibilities.

Both policemen had some knowledge of the working of automatic crossings. They knew about the reference to them in the Highway Code, they had seen at least one of the leaflets produced by BR when an automatic crossing was installed, and they had also seen the 1966 Requirements of the Ministry of Transport. One of them had attended a police driving course in 1964 and received full marks for his answer regarding the working of these crossings, but he had forgotten it all by 1968. So it was no surprise that they were completely taken aback by the brisk operation of the barriers. Remarkably, they had not seen the Emergency Notice at the level crossing and knew nothing of the telephone, despite the fact that they had passed up and down Station Road three times immediately before the accident.

At the time of the accident there were at least six other automatic crossings in North Staffordshire. Leaflets relating to each new crossing were sent to County Police HQ by BR, and to

Left: Quiet rural branch lines, where train speeds and road-traffic levels are low, may be suitable for a simplified form of crossing which has neither flashing road-traffic signals nor barriers. Such crossings are known as open crossings, which trains are allowed to approach at 10mph and pass over without stopping if the crossing is clear. This shows the Trenant Road crossing, on the Liskeard–Looe branch, where there was a compulsory stop for road traffic when this photograph was taken on 18 August 1977, at which time there were 110 open crossings on BR. Among other modifications, the 'Stop' sign was replaced by a 'Give Way' following the implementation of the revised 'Requirements' in 1981. *T. G. Flinders*

Right: A gated level crossing at Foxfield on the Cumbrian Coast line, pictured on 6 October 1984. The DMUs may have passed into history, but the crossing remains the same, controlled from the adjacent signalbox. *Rod Muncey*

local police stations. The police were usually present at site meetings and they attended automatic level crossings when a failure of equipment delayed road traffic. But, more significantly, Police Inspector Wilkes had been present at a site meeting at Hixon on 12 January 1966, preparatory to the authorisation of the level crossing, and he submitted a full report to the Chief Constable, including the working of the crossing. So the information needed to avoid a collision at Hixon was widely available in police circles, but no one appears to have taken much notice. Once again, 'The penny did not drop'.

British Railways (BR)

It was clearly the responsibility of BR to ensure safety at an automatic crossing as far as it could, and that extended to specially informing firms which carried exceptional loads about the timing cycle and the vital nature of the instruction to telephone the signalman before crossing. BR certainly knew about the use of Hixon crossing by abnormal loads, because it had widened the crossing to enable them to pass, but it failed to ensure that Robert Wynn's knew about the vital need to telephone the signalman before crossing and that it appreciated the reason for doing so. And, of course, that it instructed its drivers. BR's Engineering Department dealt with the special route orders but did so only in respect of railway bridges and made no mention of the risks at automatic crossings, which could have been included in the 'cautions' in the order in respect of the vital need to telephone the signalman before crossing.

But even then, reliance would have had to be placed on the drivers of abnormal loads actually using the telephone. The signalmen at Colwich and Meaford said that no one had ever telephoned in respect of any exceptional or heavy load before the disaster, despite several abnormal loads passing over the crossing. Even at Leominster, where there had actually been a collision and where there was a considerable volume of heavy industrial traffic, there had been no such telephone calls. The non-observance of the Exceptional Notice was quite frightening and should have sounded warning bells within the BR organisation.

Mr Gibbens' conclusions on the causes and circumstances of the Hixon accident

The real cause of the disaster was ignorance, born of a lack of imagination and foresight at the sources where one would expect to find them. Those on the scene of the accident were mainly victims of shortcomings at more responsible levels, but Mr Groves (driver of the transporter) did not appear to think about what he was doing when he negotiated the crossing, and he ought not to have risked becoming immobilised across the railway for an indefinite time. But he had not the advantage of guidance from his employers as to the inherent risks, and of the proper procedure to be adopted. The failure of his employers, Robert Wynn & Sons Ltd, was the principal factor contributing to the disaster.

The police department, from top to bottom, failed to appreciate the implications of the brisk operation of automatic crossings, even though the information existed within the force, but the Ministry of Transport had not given it a proper briefing. The Ministry was also wrong when it decided that no caution relating to automatic crossings should be included in special route orders.

British Railways' contributions to the accident were its failure to inform Robert Wynn & Sons Ltd of the vital need to telephone the signalman before using the crossing, and its failure to inform heavy hauliers generally. BR relied upon the Emergency Notice, and upon drivers reading it, which might be regarded as not 100% safe. Mr Groves did not read the notice, nor did his assistant driver. Neither even saw the headroom notice. They were oblivious of both.

There were so many opportunities in various organisations, and by various people, to avoid this accident. None was taken, and 11 people were killed as a result.

The main recommendations of the inquiry

The principal recommendations of the inquiry were as follows:

1 Conversion of crossings to automatic working should be pressed forward at greater speed.

Left: Just south of Stirling an up passenger train headed by a Class 24 diesel is seen from the cab of a down train approaching a level crossing on 28 August 1973. Well equipped with gates, wicket gates and signals, the crossing appears to be worked by crossing keepers. *Derek Cross*

2 The time before the fastest train can arrive at a crossing should be extended from 24 to 32 seconds.

3 If a second train should reach the 'strike-in' point within 20 seconds after the first train 'strikes out', the barriers should remain down and the lights continue to flash.

4 Installation of separated road lanes where the road is wide enough, to discourage zigzagging.

5 Provision of a preliminary amber warning light, illuminated for five seconds.

6 More stringent standards of road profile.

In retrospect, some of the conclusions were rather unfortunate. Though Mr Gibbens endorsed the principle of automatic half-barrier crossings, they could only be installed as fast as funds and staff availability allowed. The extension of the timing cycles seems to have been based on the performance of heavy road vehicles at the time and desires to allow a more generous time margin. On the other hand, it could encourage zigzagging by impatient motorists. Both this and the 'second train coming' proposals would push back the 'strike-in' points for trains, and the associated cabling work would be costly.

Separated road lanes clearly have their point. These are only now being adopted, where there is space to do so. Preliminary

Left: A Sleaford–Lincoln DMU approaches the gated crossing at Sleaford North on 14 June 1986. *Martin Loader*

amber lights were considered desirable to bring level crossings into line with the sequence of lights that a driver would see at road junctions.

Unfortunately, Mr Gibbons failed to calculate the cost of his recommendations, or he would have discovered that they would make AHB installations too expensive. In fact, no progress was made in automating level crossings for the next 10 years, which was a tradegy.

Changes that were adopted

All the changes proposed by Mr Gibbens were adopted save No 4, which would in fact have been useful. The previous time cycle of operation of 24 seconds before a train travelling at maximum line speed could reach the crossing was extended to 37 seconds, by the addition of eight seconds after the barriers had fallen and five seconds for the amber display.

The minimum 'road open' time, recommended to be 20 seconds, was adopted but restricted to 15 seconds. There is some justification for a minimum time, but 20 seconds was thought to be excessive.

The 'strike-in' point was now set at 52 seconds to provide for the minimum road-open time and the 'second train coming' additional time, a big increase over the then existing 24 seconds, with a corresponding increase in cabling costs and in the complexity of the system.

Other cost increases resulted from improvements in road profile and the provision of lay-bys both approaching and beyond the crossing, on both sides of the road. Together with additional telephones, the cost was high.

For several years technical resources were devoted to incorporating the new Requirements in the existing 207 automatic half-barrier crossings, and it was almost impossible to make a viable financial case for the conversion of other level crossings from gates to AHBs. Mr Gibbens' recommendation that the conversion of level crossings should be pressed forward with all speed proved almost impossible to achieve, because his other recommendations had made it financially unachievable.

Finally

Mr Gibbens made some very prescient comments in his report. He said that we must beware of judgements made with the benefit of hindsight, and he also commented that:

'Safety can in a sense be bought like any tangible commodity – the higher the price paid, the better the safety; and, in assessing the degree of safety to be acquired, one must put into the balance, on the one side, the magnitude of the danger to be eliminated and, on the other, the sacrifice in money, time, convenience, material resources *(and the neglect of other pressing safety needs elsewhere* [author's italics] involved in eliminating that danger. There is no such thing as unbounded resources for every desirable reform.'

He also drew attention to an old, but still extant, rule in the BR Rule Book, No 107(b), viz:

'Stationmasters must .... request users of traction or other heavy engines in their neighbourhood to give reasonable notice .... on each occasion of their intention to pass such engines over the line at apublic level crossing not protected with fixed signals.'

Thus the problem had been well known for a long time, dating back to the 19th century. Unfortunately, there was no longer a stationmaster at Hixon.

The ultimate solution

The possibility of replacing the automatic half barriers at Hixon by a safer form of protection began to be seriously considered. A full-barrier crossing, remotely operated, and monitored by CCTV, began to be considered but the cost of installing such a system was £1.3 million. The topography, the nature of the road and the open nature of the site allowed consideration to be given to the provision of a bridge and the closure of the level crossing. It was found to be little more expensive, at £1.6 million, than a CCTV installation, and would allow the closure of the level crossing with consequent savings.

It was the obvious solution, and a bridge was built, but not before another 30 years had passed and a further fatality had occurred at the same crossing.

Right: Traincrew-operated gates at Swavesey, on the erstwhile Cambridge–St Ives line. Southern Region Class 73/0 electro-diesel No 73 003 pauses with the 'West Anglian Enterprise' special of 30 September 1989. *L. A. Nixon*

STAGNATION, 1968-78

6

The Hixon report is published

The Hixon report was studied carefully by British Railways, with consideration being directed particularly at the recommendations. Fortunately, there were not too many of them, but the implications were clear. The existing 207 automatic half-barrier level crossings would have to be modified before any further crossings could be automated, and this would be both costly and absorb scarce technical resources. It was also clear that the process would take several years. The effect can be seen in the following table of public level crossings year by year.

Year	1968	1969	1970	1971	1972
Manned, with gates/barriers	1,936	1,896	1,731	1,602	1,558
Automatic half barriers	201	198	197	198	203
Unmanned, with gates/barriers	72	30	34	33	34
Unmanned, with gates/barriers and warning lights	31	36	39	39	38
Others	87	86	84	91	98

Year	1973	1974	1975	1976	1977	1978	1979
Manned, with gates	1,394	1,334	1,269	1,196	1,123	1,070	998
Automatic half harriers	223	233	224	229	233	234	233
Unmanned, with barriers and CCTV	29	42	64	75	97	119	139
Manned, with barriers	262	292	330	336	401	409	416
Unmanned, with gates/barriers and red/green lights	65	66	71	78	88	90	91

Below: An electric multiple-unit passes over the automatic half-barrier level crossing at Ripe, between Polegate and Lewes, in July 1970. The crossing has been fully modified to conform to the new post-Hixon safety standards and includes an amber light to give warning of the imminent operation of the flashing red road-traffic signals, an illuminated 'Another Train Coming' sign and push-button telephones at the crossing, whilst large signs on the approach to the crossing give instructions to drivers of large or slow vehicles. *BR*

Right: A gated crossing at Woodcroft, a few miles north of Peterborough on the 125mph East Coast main line, pictured on 27 September 2007. The crossing is staffed by non-resident crossing keepers who telephone the signalman for permission to open the gates to allow road traffic to cross. At this location there are five lines of way, the up and down Stamford lines of the erstwhile Midland Railway and the down fast, up fast and up slow lines of the East Coast main line. This crossing is little used by road vehicles, because opportunities to cross between trains are very limited. At one time the former Midland lines were controlled separately by a resident crossing keeper, whose cottage can be seen through the crossing gate. *Stanley Hall*

The 50% reduction in the traditional manned, gated crossing over the 12-year period will be noted, as will the increase in manned crossings with lifting barriers instead of gates, most of them equipped with flashing red road-traffic signals. The traffic signals are a great assistance to the signalman in closing the crossing, when there are heavy flows of road traffic.

There was a very small increase in automatic half barrier crossings of only 32 in 12 years. Modifications resulting from the recommendations of the Hixon inquiry were virtually completed by the end of 1972, and technical resources were then released to allow for the introduction of further AHB installations. Not many were done owing to the high cost.

There was a new category of unmanned full-barrier crossings with interlocked railway signals, monitored remotely by CCTV. Many of these resulted from the resignalling of main trunk routes and would not in many cases have been suitable for AHB installations.

A second new category, not listed above, was that of unmanned crossings without gates or barriers but with road-traffic signals, known as AOCL (automatic open crossings locally monitored). There were 84 of these in 1979.

In 1968 there were 2,327 public-road level crossings, of which 1,936 were manned and 11 years later, in 1979, there were 1,960, with 1,414 manned. Those 1,414 manned crossings represented a

Right: A manually-controlled barrier crossing at Saltmarshe, near Goole, on the line from Hull, 25 August 1984. Note the specially-shaped corner of the signalbox, to give the signalman a clearer view of approaching road vehicles. *M. F. Haddon*

considerable challenge. AHBs were too expensive and CCTV crossings were even more expensive.

Between 1968 and 1979, 367 public-road level crossings had been closed or taken out of use, mainly through line closures or the building of bridges. The number of manned crossings had been reduced by 522, by the slight increase in AHB crossings and the new categories of CCTV crossings, AOCL crossings and MWL crossings.

The safety record at level crossings, 1969-79

The number of fatalities, year by year.

Year	1969	70	71	72	73	74	75	76	77	78	79	Totals
Manned, with gates/barriers	3	4	4	2	5	3	2	2	4	5	2	**36**
Automatic half barriers						2	1	2		3	1	**9**
Unmanned, with gates/ barriers and red/green lights							1				3	**4**
Unmanned, without gates/barriers												**0**

Of the 36 fatalities at manned gates, 20 were pedestrians, 11 were occupants of road vehicles and five were railway staff. Of the nine fatalities at AHB crossings, five were occupants of road vehicles, and four were pedestrians.

Details of some of the more notable accidents

Crossing keepers were involved in many of the accidents, emphasising the need to replace the gates with automatic half-barrier installations if an economic case could be made. In the absence of an economic case for AHBs, some cheaper, but acceptable, automatic system was needed, such as automatic open crossings (AOCLs).

In 1969 a crossing keeper at Vange Wharf, near Pitsea on the Tilbury line, irregularly left his gates open, and a lorry driver, seeing the gates open, drove on to the crossing. At the same moment a 4-coach electric multiple-unit travelling at about 50mph went on to the crossing and struck the lorry, wrecking it and killing the unfortunate driver. The first three coaches of the train were derailed, the leading coach coming to rest in a field on its side, but none of the passengers was seriously hurt.

There was a public inquiry into a fatal accident at Dowdyke gated level crossing, on the now-closed line between Spalding and Boston, on 28 January 1970. The crossing keeper opened the gates, which swung away from the railway, to allow a sewage disposal tanker to cross, without observing the duplicate block instruments, which showed a train in section. A two-car diesel multiple-unit, travelling at about 50mph, smashed into the tanker and hurled it into the side of the crossing keeper's cottage, badly damaging it. The tractor was almost totally destroyed, its driver

Below: Manually-controlled barriers at Berwick, between Lewes and Polegate, 10 June 1986. *F. W. Smith*

being injured and his mate killed. The train was derailed and severely damaged, but none of the traincrew or the six passengers was seriously hurt. The report mentioned that there were no fewer than 14 public level crossings in 6½ miles on the line.

In 1970, whilst there were no fatalities at AHB crossings, there were several cases when cars skidded on level crossings, leaving the road area and coming to rest on the cattle-cum-trespass guards, to be hit by trains. This was particularly a problem where the road had a double bend (as at Midcalder, between Carstairs and Edinburgh), or where the road crossed the railway at a skew angle (as at Upper Denton, near Haltwhistle, and Silverdale, near

Carnforth). It was not unknown for motorists to become confused on such crossings in the dark, and turn too quickly, driving along the railway line for some distance. In most cases the cars were struck by a train, but without derailment and without injuries. The cars' occupants all got out in time, but at the locations mentioned none of them used the emergency telephones to alert the signalman and have trains stopped. In one remarkable case the empty car, which had been pushed along the line for some distance by the train, was manhandled out of the way of the train by the car's occupants, assisted by the traincrew, and some of the train's passengers. This was a most unusual example of self-help.

Above: A manually-controlled barrier crossing at Churchill & Blakedown (ex-GWR), between Stourbridge Junction and Kidderminster, seen on 25 June 2007. Note the length of the barrier arms, each one of which closes the full width of the roadway and the footpath. *Stanley Hall*

Right: Manually-controlled barrier crossing at Beverley, between Hull and Driffield, 9 August 1996. *F. W. Smith*

Zigzagging around the lowered barrier at an automatic level crossing has always been a problem, but it can have serious results. In July 1973 a car with three passengers passed the lowered barrier at Newcastle Road AHB crossing (Nantwich) and was struck by a train and wrecked. All four occupants of the car were injured. Another driver had seen the car zigzag round the barrier and used the emergency telephone to warn the signalman. The reckless car driver was charged with dangerous driving and fined £30, which seems a paltry sum for endangering the lives of train passengers, traincrews and his own passengers.

In the same year, the driver of a passenger train on the 15in-gauge Romney, Hythe & Dymchurch Light Railway was killed when his locomotive was rammed and overturned on a crossing at St Mary's Road, Dymchurch, by youths driving a stolen car. The leading coach was also turned on its side. The car driver was found guilty of causing death by dangerous driving and sentenced to 18 months' imprisonment. Since then there have been two more cases of train drivers' being killed at level crossings on this narrow-gauge line when a car hit their locomotive.

In 1974 there was an unusual fatality at Littleport gated level crossing, between Ely and Downham Market. The signalman accidentally released the wicket gates after a train had passed, when another train was closely approaching on the other line. A pedestrian was killed. Wicket gates are not normally interlocked with protecting railway signals. Even the ability to lock the wicket gates to prevent access to the crossing is not entirely foolproof.

During 1975, a typical year, there were 40 accidents at gated crossings in which the gates were damaged or completely destroyed. Some of the accidents were caused by train drivers failing to stop at the protecting signals, some were caused by irregular operation of the gates by crossing keepers, and road users caused some. None of these accidents resulted in fatalities or injuries. There was one fatality at an AHB crossing when an elderly lady pushed her bicycle past the lowered barrier at Great Plumstead level crossing, on the Norwich–Cromer line.

Level crossings with miniature red and green warning lights rely for their safety upon road users' closing the gates after themselves, and misuse was not uncommon. An open gate might be regarded as an invitation to cross by some car drivers and one was slightly injured when he ignored the red light and drove on to the crossing. A train struck his car. In an attempt to overcome the problem of the gates being left open a new system was devised which consisted of a barrier, hydraulically raised by the crossing user operating a pump. The barrier on the opposite side was lowered by the simple operation of a release button. These installations were suitable for lightly used crossings and were cheaper than AHB crossings. Eventually, misuse resulted in the installation of miniature red/green warning light equipment being restricted to private road crossings.

In 1976 there were again 40 accidents at gated crossings, the same as in the previous year. A crossing keeper was killed. Plans

Right: Intermediate stage of development at Manea level crossing, between Ely and March, on 22 May 1979: manually-controlled barriers, but no road-traffic signals. *Stanley Hall*

Below: The 13.18 DMU from Nottingham to Lincoln St Marks passes over the manually-controlled barrier crossing at Sneinton Junction, Nottingham, on 25 October 1976. *L. A. Nixon*

were implemented to replace the gates at one crossing with manned barriers monitored by CCTV, a very expensive solution. At another location a bridge replaced the crossing, and elsewhere a crossing was closed and road traffic diverted over a new AHB installation nearby.

There were the usual problems at AHB crossings, with road vehicles zigzagging, and one being driven along the railway by mistake in the dark. The car was destroyed. There was a rather more worrying case in which vandals left a car on a crossing, where it was hit by a train.

By now there were 52 automatic open crossings with road-traffic signals but neither gates nor barriers. The speed of trains approaching such crossings is limited so that the train driver can stop before reaching the crossing if he sees that it is obstructed. For the third year running there had been no accidents at any of them.

However, 1976 was a significant year. No progress was being made with the installation of automatic half barriers at crossings, owing to the high cost, and neither automatic open crossings (AOCLs) nor miniature red-green warning light (MWL) crossings were seen as suitable alternatives in many cases. Automatic open crossings were suitable only on rural lines where train speeds could be reduced, and MWL equipment was not considered to be suitable at public crossings. Towards the end of the year, members of the Railway Inspectorate of the Department of Transport met officials of the British Railways Board Headquarters to see what could be done to break the log-jam of crossings suitable for conversion to AHBs. Following this meeting Lt-Col I. K. A. McNaughton, the Chief Inspecting Officer of Railways, set out the terms of reference of a proposed working party in a letter to Lt Col Townsend Rose, dated 5 January 1977. This was a very significant development.

In his letter, Col McNaughton mentioned the current situation in which efforts to improve safety at level crossings and reduce manning costs had been frustrated by the very high cost of automatic half-barrier installations, following the adoption of the revised standards (known as Requirements) incorporating Mr Gibbens' recommendations in his report on the Hixon accident. He drew attention to the almost complete lack of progress in installing AHBs because they were now too expensive and sophisticated. He noted that the Department of Transport and the British Railways Board had agreed to set up a Working Party and he suggested the following aim:

'To consider ways in which methods of level crossing protection can be further developed in Great Britain, taking into account the cost and the need to maintain an adequate and publicly acceptable standard of safety – and to make recommendations.'

The activities of the Working Party, which largely governed level-crossing policies for the next 30 years, will be examined and discussed in the next chapter.

Accidents, 1977-9

Somewhat ironically, 1977 was a good year, and there were only four fatalities, all occupants of road vehicles. That year 87 new full-barrier installations were commissioned, 73 of them being in place of gates, and there were no accidents at any crossings of this type, emphasising the high standard of safety of full-barrier crossings.

Three of the four fatalities were caused by crossing keepers, giving the Working Party mentioned above an incentive to eliminate this type of crossing. The fourth fatal accident was at Burnt House, Cantley, on the Norwich–Lowestoft line, when a motor cyclist pushed his machine through the wicket gates (which had no locking mechanism) and was killed by a passenger train. He had previously been warned of the danger.

One of the fatalities occurred in unusual circumstances on a freight-only crossing at Rawtenstall when a car was driven into the side of a train passing over the crossing. The crossing keeper had failed to close the gate (although the train might be thought to have provided a much greater visual impact than the gate) and unusually for those days he was charged with manslaughter, but was discharged. The train driver was also charged with manslaughter, and having pleaded not guilty to that charge he pleaded guilty to endangering the safety of persons on the railway and was fined £50.

Silverdale AHB crossing, between Carnforth and Arnside, was again in the news when a car failed to negotiate the 'S' bend in the road and was struck by a passenger train. The occupants had managed to get clear. One of the problems at this crossing is the slight rising gradient of the road on both sides of the crossing, which has the effect of preventing the road user from being able to see the road and rail layout in advance. There had been similar incidents in January 1976, January and December 1977 and again January and March 1978. Most of them occurred after dark, and after the last occasion the road markings and signs were improved. Even as late as 2007 there were still problems at this level crossing. The only effective answer would be to modify the road layout and move the sharp right-hand bend further away from the crossing, but this would be expensive.

At a number of locations there is a station on the approach side, and adjacent to, an AHB crossing, and there is a railway signal at the departure end of the platform. Trains are allowed to enter the station with the signal at Danger and the level crossing barriers in the raised position, allowing road traffic to continue to cross. When the train has stopped and is ready to depart, the guard presses a plunger, which initiates the crossing sequence. The

railway signal does not clear to green until the crossing sequence is complete. The purpose of this arrangement is to avoid the delays to road traffic, and the increased risk of zigzagging, if the normal full automatic sequence were in operation. However, the system depends on the train driver actually stopping at the signal and at Milford station, near Godalming, on 22 December 1978 he failed to do so, killing a car driver. At some locations the method of operation of the barriers can be selected by the signalman to allow automatic or non-automatic mode, known as non-stopping/stopping selection.

The most serious accident in 1979 occurred on 13 March at Naas level crossing, on the Newport–Gloucester line. This is a lightly-used crossing and was equipped with hydraulically-operated lifting barriers and miniature red and green warning lights on 23 October 1970. A large lorry, an 8-wheeled Scammell carrying a skip loaded with 10 tons of refuse, and with a total loaded weight of 25 tons, was being driven over the crossing when it was hit at 60mph by a 10-coach express passenger train headed by a diesel-electric locomotive. The lorry was largely demolished and its driver killed. The train was not derailed, but the driving cab of the locomotive was completely crushed, killing the two locomen on board. There had been growing concern about the suitability of miniature warning lights at public level crossings and it had already been decided that there should be no new installations on public roads. They were thought, however, to continue to be suitable for use at private crossings.

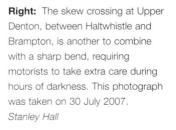

Above: A motorist approaches the lowered half barrier at Silverdale crossing just in time to witness the passage of Class 40 No 40 141 at the head of the 12.22 Sellafield–Bridgwater nuclear flask train on 12 July 1983. This crossing is on a sharply-skewed angle which occasionally confuses motorists.
Paul Shannon

Right: The skew crossing at Upper Denton, between Haltwhistle and Brampton, is another to combine with a sharp bend, requiring motorists to take extra care during hours of darkness. This photograph was taken on 30 July 2007.
Stanley Hall

Above: A Southern Region 'Tadpole' DEMU forming the 16.45 Ashford–Hastings service passes over the level crossing at Appledore on 27 July 1982. The gates have since been replaced by automatic half barriers. *Colin J. Marsden*

Left: One of the early experiments with miniature warning lights and user-operated lifting barriers, at Back Lane crossing (between Trent Sheet Stores Junction and Stenson Junction), recorded in February 1970. A pump handle had to be operated to raise the barriers, but they were lowered by holding down a 'Release' lever. However, road users sometimes couldn't be bothered to lower the barriers; indeed, they possibly thought it didn't really matter, but this could send a dangerously misleading message to the next road user, and for this reason the use of crossings with miniature warning lights was discontinued on public roads. *BR*

Above: In 1969 holiday trains still ran from the West Riding to Bridlington. Here Class 45 'Peak' No 74 passes Cherry Tree signalbox and manually-controlled barrier crossing on Saturday 5 July. Nowadays the barriers are worked remotely from Beverley signalbox and monitored by CCTV. *G. J. Holt*

Above and left: Low Row signalbox and level crossing, on the line between Haltwhistle and Carlisle, pictured 30 July 2007. The crossing has electrically-powered swinging boom gates. *Stanley Hall*

Left and below: A new type of open level crossing (*i.e.* no gates or barriers) was installed at Naas, near Lydney, between Newport and Gloucester, following the serious accident there on 13 March 1979. This type of level crossing was authorised following the 1978 Review and has automatic amber and flashing red road-traffic signals, with a 'warbler' for pedestrians. If a second train is coming the warnings are supplemented by an 'Another Train Coming' flashing red signal, and the tone of the warbler changes. The equipment is monitored in the supervising signalbox (Newport), and telephones to the signalbox are provided at the crossing. The crossings are known as automatic open crossings remotely monitored (AOCR), considered suitable for lines with train speeds of up to 75mph. These photographs date from 30 June 1983. *BR*

7

A NEW DAWN BREAKS

A Major Reappraisal of Level Crossing Policy after 1978

The Working Party goes on a wide-ranging tour of Western Europe

The Working Party consisted of the following members:

Lt-Col A. G. Townsend-Rose, Inspecting Officer of Railways, Department of Transport, Joint Chairman

F. C. Walmsley — Signalling Officer, Chief Operations Manager's Department, British Railways Board, Joint Chairman

For the Department of Transport:

B. A. Payne — Railways Directorate
C. J. Harris — Railways Directorate
F. E. C. Habgood — Traffic Engineering Division
N. E. Metcalfe — Road Safety Directorate

For the British Railways Board:

K. E. Hodgson — Chief Signal and Telecommunications Engineer's Department
T. W. Craig — Chief Signal and Telecommunications Engineer's Department

The Working Party visited France, Holland, West Germany and Switzerland between 20 and 25 March 1977 and on 17 and 18 October 1977 and found that the modernisation and automation of level crossings in those countries had been proceeding on a large scale for many years. As a result of this experience, and an earnest desire to make some progress in Britain, they made the following recommendations:

Automatic half barriers (AHBs)

The installation of automatic half barriers at level crossings and the withdrawal of manning had been proceeding apace before the Hixon accident. It was seen to have had several advantages, which have already been discussed. But the increased cost of AHBs incorporating the Hixon recommendations had made them unaffordable, and one of the main aims of the Working Party was to review those recommendations, drawing on Continental experience, and if practicable to reduce the cost of AHBs to an affordable level, so that progress could be resumed.

The amber aspect

Only in Britain are the flashing red road-traffic signals preceded by an amber aspect. However, it was decided to retain this feature as it matches normal highway practice, but the period during which the amber aspect is shown should be reduced from five seconds to three seconds.

Below: Class 66 diesel locomotive No 66 191 heads a train of china-clay wagons over the manually-controlled barrier crossing at Lostwithiel in May 2000. *Stanley Hall*

The operating-time cycle

The minimum time cycle in Britain of 37 seconds is considerably longer than in most other countries. Experience had given no justification for the increased time following Hixon, and a return to the pre-Hixon time of 24 seconds was recommended.

'Road Open' periods

Only in Britain is there a system of outer control which provides for a minimum 'road-open' period, together with a special illuminated sign to warn motorists that another train is coming. The 'road-open' time was fixed at 15 seconds post-Hixon, and whilst it was felt by the Working Party that there should be a 'road-open' period, they decided that 10 seconds would be sufficient. The special illuminated 'Another Train Coming' sign introduced post-Hixon was an expensive flashing neon sign and it was decided to discontinue its use and replace it with a fixed sign.

Road Profile

Only in Britain are there such stringent requirements relating to road profiles over the crossing, which might be considered an over-reaction to Hixon. Revised profile standards were set.

Telephones at level crossings

These allow communication with the supervising signalbox and are not provided in any other country except France, and then only at busy crossings. However, the Working Party felt that they

served a useful, and sometimes vital, purpose in Britain, but the present number of six at each AHB crossing was excessive and should be reduced to two.

Abnormal vehicles

Only in Britain are there special arrangements for dealing with unusually large or slow vehicles. All these points of difference came about as a result of the Hixon recommendations, and it was recommended that the practice of providing special lay-bys and telephones on each side of the road, both approaching and beyond the crossing, should be abandoned. Special signs should be erected for the guidance of drivers of abnormal vehicles.

The proposed introduction of automatic open crossings

Even when all these relaxations in the conditions for AHBs had been adopted, standards in Britain would still be more onerous than on the Continent, but the Working Party felt that AHBs might now be affordable without compromising safety, and that the quicker operating-cycle time would provide less of a temptation to zigzag.

Whilst AHBs were the main focus of the visit, it was well known that there were many crossings on more lightly-used lines where even the lower expected cost of AHBs would still not be viable. Automatic open crossings were proposed to cover this situation, and two types were proposed:

Automatic open crossings remotely monitored (AOCR)

The Working Party made a very thorough study of automatic open crossings with road-traffic signals in Europe, where many hundreds have been installed, often with little or no remote monitoring of the correct operation of the road-traffic signals. They noted also that such crossings were often installed on lines with speeds up to 100mph, and concluded that there could be scope for such crossings in Britain.

The Working Party envisaged an installation similar in many respects to an AHB crossing without the half barriers, but wished to proceed cautiously until some experience had been gained. It would be cheaper than an AHB crossing and could provide an alternative at locations where an AHB was not viable.

It was decided that the maximum line speed should be 75mph and that the mix of train frequency and the volume of road traffic should be restricted as follows. The maximum road volume should not exceed 2,000 vehicles during the period 6.0am to midnight and the traffic moment during that period should not exceed 40,000 (traffic moment is obtained by multiplying the number of trains by the number of road vehicles). In terms of cold statistics, the traffic moment of 40,000 would reduce the chance of a train and a road vehicle meeting on the crossing at the same precise moment, and so reduce the chance of a collision (or extend the time before one inevitably happened). There were some reservations in the Working Party about AOCRs on safety grounds, but it was agreed to have some trial sites.

The basic time cycle would be 27 seconds from 'strike-in' and there would be a minimum 'road-open' period of 10 seconds. The operation of the road-traffic signals would be monitored from the supervising signalbox and a telephone to that signalbox would be provided at each side of the crossing.

Automatic open crossings locally monitored (AOCL)

AOCL crossings were first introduced in 1963. They have the usual flashing red road-traffic signals, and train speeds over the crossing limited to a maximum of 35mph, being lower than that according to the density of road traffic. The operation of the road-traffic signals is monitored by the train driver, who is instructed to stop short of the crossing if a white flashing light signal, generally placed just before the crossing, does not show as the train approaches. The driver may then pass over the crossing cautiously. The train driver must also be prepared to stop his train short of the crossing if he sees it to be obstructed when it comes into view. No telephones are provided. These crossings are self-contained and are therefore much cheaper than AHB and AOCR crossings.

However, the low train speeds limited the suitability of such crossings, and only 58 had been installed by the end of 1977. They had an excellent safety record, which was one of the factors causing the Working Party to consider how they could be more widely used. They recommended that the maximum train speed over an AOCL crossing should be related to the braking distance from which the driver can have a satisfactory view of the crossing.

Left and middle: Around the village of Denton, between Haltwhistle and Carlisle, no fewer than six level crossings of various types are to be found within a little over a mile. These two photographs, taken on 30 July 2007, feature two of them, Denton School and Upper Denton — both automatic half-barrier installations, and both at a pronounced skew angle. Notice the unusual vertical arrangement of the offside road-traffic signals at the latter, to improve visibility. *Stanley Hall*

Left: Denton School crossing, seen on 26 July 1979, when it was still a manned, gated crossing. Notice the very tall gateposts, necessary to provide extra support to the very long single gates. *Stanley Hall*

This would be about 600yd, with a potential crossing speed of about 55mph. The basic operating time cycle should be 27 seconds (3 seconds amber and 24 seconds flashing red), with a minimum 'road-open' period of 10 seconds before the cycle restarted for a train from the opposite direction. A flashing warning sign should be provided to warn road vehicle drivers that another train was approaching, with an audible warning for pedestrians.

The crossing should be illuminated during darkness, with the lights being switched on as soon as the road-traffic signals began to show for an approaching train, to enable its driver to check if the crossing is clear. No telephones would be provided, but the telephone number of a supervising point would be given.

The cost advantages of automatic open crossings over half-barrier crossings are affected by the road-width requirements. An AHB crossing requires that the exit from the crossing must always be open so that there is no risk that a road vehicle driver will be trapped on the crossing. In consequence, an AHB crossing can only be installed where the road is sufficiently wide to allow this. Widening the road to provide sufficient width for an AHB can be very expensive even if physically possible. Such widening of a narrow road over the crossing would also create a passing place on the crossing itself where traffic in one direction might stop to allow vehicles coming the other way to pass – an obvious danger. Automatic open crossings could be installed on narrower roads than AHB crossings.

Above: A pre-electrification view of Helpston level crossing, five miles north of Peterborough, with Class 47/4 diesel No 47 591 heading the 07.17 'European' express from Parkeston Quay to Edinburgh and Glasgow on 19 November 1983. In the foreground are the former Midland lines, while beyond the signalbox are the East Coast fast and slow lines. The erstwhile Midland signalbox has been demolished, and the ex-GNR 'box now controls what must be one of the longest — and busiest — level crossings in Britain. *John C. Baker*

Right: A more recent view of Helpston level crossing, recorded on 27 September 2007. Electrification aside, little has changed, but there are now many more expresses using the line. *Stanley Hall*

Miniature warning lights

These were devised to provide a positive warning of approaching trains at user-operated crossings, and rely on the user to respond to the miniature red/green warning light signals and the associated notice boards. The light signals are operated by approaching trains. They began to be installed in the late 1960s and by 1978 there were 88 crossings equipped with miniature warning lights, 45 of them on public roads and 43 at private crossings. Gates were provided at 78 of these crossings, with lightweight barriers being provided at the other 10. The accident rate was very low, but indiscipline among road users in leaving the gates open or the barriers raised after use caused the BRB to decide not to install any more on public roads. Subsequently they have found increasing use at private crossings and at footpath and bridleway crossings on main lines where train speeds are high or the view of approaching trains is poor.

Open crossings

These crossings are mainly to be found on lightly-used roads where train speeds over the crossing can be limited to 10mph. Road signs require road traffic to 'Give Way' to trains. They are limited to a maximum daily traffic moment of 2,000 (e.g. 10 trains and 200 road vehicles). In 1978 there were 107 of these crossings; in 2005 there were 58.

The introduction of the new arrangements

The new standards were incorporated in a Department of Transport booklet entitled 'Railway Construction and Operation Requirements, Level Crossings', and came into force in 1981. However, both the British Railways Board and the Department of Transport were anxious to make progress and the first 'new look' AHB was installed at Doddington Road, Lincoln, in March 1980. A second crossing was installed later that year. The effect on the rate of modernisation of level crossings is shown below, compared with the detail shown in the previous chapter.

Year	1981	82	83	84	85	86	87	88	89	90
Manned, with barriers	432	423	403	394	363	338	326	321	321	320
Manned, with barriers and CCTV	168	184	194	201	220	228	251	258	264	275
Manned, with gates	871	802	735	657	576	468	452	473	440	383
Automatic half barriers	250	255	267	280	291	315	323	357	398	412
AOCR	0	0	8	25	39	44	44	33	14	8
AOCL	114	122	128	144	188	206	206	211	211	206

Notes

The 25% decrease in manned barrier crossings resulted mainly from their conversion to unmanned barrier crossings monitored by CCTV.

The number of traditional manned crossings with gates was reduced by well over half, with a corresponding increase of 162 in automatic half-barrier crossings and of 92 in AOCL crossings.

During the 10-year period, over 200 crossings were closed completely, some being replaced by bridges.

There was a rapid increase in AOCL crossings until 1986, which came almost to a stand following the Lockington Report, described below.

Right: The first of four views of the crossing at Silverdale, between Carnforth and Arnside, recorded on 10 July 2007. There are six signs here, plus the normal initial signs and the signs at the crossing itself. In this photograph the barriers are down for a Class 175 DMU heading towards Barrow. The 'S' bend and 'Reduce speed' signs are recent, non-standard additions. *Stanley Hall*

Below left and right: The skew nature of the crossing, with a sharp bend in the road immediately beyond, has led some motorists to turn too quickly on wet, dark nights and proceed along the railway line. Illustrating the point are these two photographs taken in the direction of Barrow. *Stanley Hall (both)*

There was a quite rapid increase in automatic open crossings (remotely monitored) until 1986, which was almost completely reversed following the Lockington Report.

It was very disappointing to find that by 1990 there were still 383 manned, gated crossings, and even more disappointing to find that 15 years later there were still 253.

The Lockington accident in 1986 had a very similar effect to the Hixon accident; it is described in detail in the next chapter. The confidence in open crossings in the 1978 Working Party report was brought into question, and not only were no further AOCR installations brought into use, but also all except one were converted mainly to automatic half-barrier crossings. And there were few more AOCLs. Their accident record had not been good, although owing to the generally low train speeds involved the results were less serious, and it was not felt necessary to convert them to other types of crossing.

Perhaps the greatest disappointment concerned the relatively slow progress in increasing the number of automatic half-barrier

crossings. There was less than one new installation per month until the urgent need to convert AOCR crossings to AHB crossings increased the rate of progress. The Working Party had confidently envisaged several hundred new AHB installations, but it never happened. During the 1990s, only 53 more AHB installations were brought into use and the number has remained almost static since then. The increase in train speeds and the greater demands for safety both generally and at level crossings have led to the AHB crossing being less highly regarded than previously.

The safety of pedestrians at public level crossings – the Oppenheim Committee

In 1982 there was some concern in Parliament about the safety of pedestrians at public level crossings, and the Department of Transport held an inquiry, chaired by Dame Sally Oppenheim-Barnes PC. The concern was largely unfounded, when one considers the small number of fatalities and injuries suffered by pedestrians at public level crossings. In the 10-year period 1972-81 there were 19 fatalities and eight persons injured, of which 14 fatalities and five injuries took place at manned crossings with

Left: 'Sharp Bend' warning signs have been erected. The lamp and warbler on the pole at the centre of the photograph have been provided to alert pedestrians that the crossing equipment has been activated and they need to hurry, or remain where they are, because the barrier arm will begin to descend in about 10 seconds. *Stanley Hall*

gates. In 1972 there were 1,362 manned gated crossings, but by 1981 the figure had gone down to 871. The British Railways Board prepared a memorandum on the subject for consideration by the inquiry. It was noticeable that at public meetings held as part of the consultation process on modernising a level crossing, one of the issues that was always raised was the safety of AHB crossings for children. There was no evidence to support such fears but they were understandable. BR always undertook extensive publicity campaigns, especially directed at schools.

'A Report by the Committee of Inquiry into Pedestrian Safety at Public Level Crossings' was published in April 1983, its main conclusion being that automatic level crossings were no less safe

Below: Black Dyke automatic half-barrier crossing, near Arnside, approached on a sharp bend in the road. The photograph was taken on 10 July 2007. *Stanley Hall*

Level Crossings

than the gated crossings they replaced, so far as pedestrians were concerned. However, it said that experience had shown that a few minor changes in detail of the Requirements for Level Crossings might be beneficial. It is difficult to see what all the fuss was about – there had been only five fatalities at AHB crossings in the 10 years preceding the report.

The records do not differentiate between crossings with separate pedestrian gates and those without pedestrian gates, nor between crossings with gates which alternately close against the roadway and then against the railway, and those with field gates which open away from the railway. Most pedestrian gates were capable of being locked by the signalman or crossing keeper, but some had no lock. The causes of accident varied. Sometimes the signalman or crossing keeper was at fault. In some cases the act of crossing behind one train and being stuck by one coming the other way was the cause. At some crossings, miniature red/green lights had been provided to help the pedestrian cross safely, but they were only effective if they were obeyed, which unfortunately was not always the case.

The safest crossings were those with barriers which closed the whole roadway and did not have separate pedestrian access, but this penalised those pedestrians who, with care, could have crossed

safely until the train was closer to the crossing. It is, of course, not unknown for pedestrians to find themselves trapped between the barriers at full-barrier crossings when they have started to cross with the barriers are already falling, but their predicament will be apparent to the signalman monitoring the crossing, who will not allow a train to approach until it is safe to do so.

Accidents, 1981-90

Zigzagging around lowered half barriers continued to be a source of accident. On 5 March 1981 a car was driven at speed into the side of a passing train at Riccall Turnhead AHB, on the now-closed section of the East Coast main line between Selby and York, killing the car driver and seriously injuring his passenger. The whole episode was witnessed by an off-duty policeman waiting in his car at the crossing.

The latest in a long line of accidents at Silverdale AHB crossing, near Carnforth, occurred on 22 January 1982, when a motorist drove on to the crossing past the flashing red road-traffic signals and the lowered half barrier, and was killed when his car was hit by a light locomotive. There was another zigzagging fatality that year, at Broom Lane AHB crossing, between Syston and Melton Mowbray, when a car was hit by a freight train. Whilst such motorists pay the penalty for their own folly, the train driver can only cling on and hope that his train will not be derailed.

There were four accidents in 1982 at automatic open crossings locally monitored. In one a double-decker bus followed a car onto a crossing at Netherfield Lane, near Nottingham, and was struck by a freight train travelling at low speed.

In 1983 there were two accidents in unusual circumstances at AHB crossings. On 18 August a stolen car being pursued by the police crashed through the lowered barriers at Burrows Lane (Gomshall), between Guildford and Dorking, where it was struck by a diesel multiple-unit. The car driver was killed. On 21 December, at Spronces crossing, Attleborough, a car became stuck on the cattle guards when its driver tried to turn it round on the crossing. It was struck by trains in both directions but the car driver was unharmed. He had left his car to telephone the signalman, but did not do so until the lights started to flash, which was too late.

In 1984 automatic half-barrier crossings again featured in the more serious accidents. There was a particularly bad one at Pooley Green AHB crossing, Egham, when the driver of a car second in line in a queue at the crossing pulled out and drove onto the crossing. There were five people in the car, three being killed and two injured when the car was struck by an electric multiple-unit train.

Zigzagging around the barriers continued to result in deaths of car drivers and their passengers. At Dean Hill AHB crossing, between Salisbury and Romsey, a car was hit by a freight train, killing one of its passengers and injuring five other occupants. The car driver was jailed for a month and banned from driving for four

Below: A newly-installed automatic open crossing locally monitored (AOCL) at Seaton Bank Head, photographed on 27 May 1984. The road-traffic signals are operated automatically by an approaching train and are monitored by the train driver, who approaches the crossing at restricted speed and checks that it is not obstructed. Note that the track has been singled. *Ian S. Carr*

years. Two brothers were killed in their lorry when they tried to beat a freight train over an AHB crossing at Linwith Lane, on the branch to Drax power station, between Knottingley and Goole. They had miscalculated and paid the penalty.

In 1986 there was an accident of a significant nature when a car driver was killed. His car was struck by an electric multiple-unit at King's Fernsden AHB crossing. The train was derailed but there were no injuries to its passengers. A verdict of suicide was returned by the Coroner, an unusual development.

Three car drivers were killed in separate zigzagging incidents when their cars were struck by trains on AHB level crossings. A train driver was injured in one of the incidents.

The annual increase in the number of automatic open crossings remotely monitored (AOCR) was bound eventually to increase the likelihood of fatal accidents, and there were three in 1986. Lockington was one, and the others were at Pulford, between Wrexham and Chester, in which a passenger in a minibus was killed when the vehicle was struck by a diesel multiple-unit, and a car driver was killed when his vehicle was struck by a train at St Germans crossing, between Downham Market and King's Lynn. Both road vehicle drivers had failed to observe, or obey, the flashing red road-traffic signals. The optimism shown for this type of crossing in the 1978 Working Party report was coming to be questioned. There were also two separate fatal accidents at AOCL crossings, raising a question mark against that type of crossing too.

In 1987 the melancholy tale of zigzagging deaths at automatic half-barrier level crossings continued, when a teenage driver and his passenger were killed after their car was struck on Rearsby AHB crossing, between Syston and Melton Mowbray. There were two other similar incidents, but without fatalities. It was becoming clear that without zigzagging incidents, AHB crossings had a very good safety record.

The year 1988 followed much the same pattern. There were six deaths at manual and automatic crossings, five of which were occupants of road vehicles and one a pedestrian. Two of the deaths were at automatic half-barrier crossings, both being caused as usual by motorists zigzagging, reinforcing the view that without such behaviour AHB crossings are very safe.

There were two deaths at automatic open crossings, one being a pedestrian at an AOCR. In neither case were the road-traffic signals obeyed. Failure to observe and obey the road-traffic signals was becoming a feature of open crossings and it was felt that the present situation was unsatisfactory. It was clear that more needed to be done to make the crossings more visually arresting to road users, and a simple way to achieve this would be to add a half barrier, whilst retaining all the existing features of an automatic open crossing. So far as the motorist was concerned, such modified crossings would be identical to standard AHB crossings and would be known as automatic barrier crossings locally monitored (ABCL). A prototype was installed at Beccles and was undergoing service trials.

It was expected that AOCR crossings would be phased out in two or three years, being converted to AHB, AOCL or ABCL crossings. The new ABCLs would then be applied to some of the AOCL crossings in order to upgrade them. It remained to be seen whether zigzagging would be a problem at ABCL crossings, with the lower train speeds possibly encouraging such behaviour. There appear to be no records of the frequency at which vehicles were driven over open crossings when the road-traffic signals were flashing, nor whether the cause was accidental or deliberate.

And so another of the 1977 Working Party's bold and ambitious proposals was killed off by the behaviour of a small minority of road users, but the BRB could not allow the lives of rail passengers and staff to be put at risk by recklessness or carelessness.

The year of 1989 was better. No one was killed at any of the automatic crossings except for two occupants of a road vehicle struck by a DMU at Bramfield AOCL crossing, near Halesworth, on the East Suffolk line. However, two occupants of a car were killed at Back Lane MWL crossing, between Trent and Castle Donington, when their vehicle was hit by a locomotive-hauled train. The user-operated barriers had been left in the raised position by the previous user, and might have been taken as an implied invitation to cross. This was the inherent danger of MWL crossings and led to their use on public roads being discontinued. They are, however, increasingly used at private road crossings where the usage might be considered local, and at some footpath and bridleway crossings.

There was only one fatality in a train/vehicle collision at a public level crossing in 1990, although the driver and his two passengers were injured when their car was driven round the barriers at an AHB crossing at Habrough, on the Barnetby–Cleethorpes line.

And so the decade ended on a favourable note. Only eight AOCR crossings remained.

Right: On 1 August 1983 an automatic open crossing locally monitored (AOCL) on the line between Battersby and Middlesbrough receives a distinguished visitor in the form of preserved ex-LMS 'Jubilee' No 5690 *Leander*. For once the pictorial part of the sign is accurate, on account of the locomotive's 4-6-0 wheel arrangement! *Bob Avery*

THE LOCKINGTON DISASTER AND ITS AFTERMATH

8

Circumstances of the accident

Saturday 26 July 1986 was a fine, sunny day on the East Coast of Yorkshire. In Bridlington station the 09.33 stopping train to Hull, formed of a pair of two-car diesel multiple-units, was loading up with holidaymakers on their way home. None had any apprehension of possible danger in the relatively short journey ahead; after all, this was a quiet line with no high speeds so why should there be any cause for concern? The train left Bridlington on time with about 120 passengers on board, and set off on its routine 31 mile, 49 min journey. At 09.55 it called at Hutton Cranswick station and after a short pause it went on its way again. Nothing could have been more normal.

Three miles further down the line, at the closed station of Lockington, everything was normal too. One of the occupants of the railway cottages behind the station saw her next-door neighbour climb into his blue Ford Escort van, taking his small son and a dog with him as he did every Saturday morning, and set off towards the lane at the exit from the station yard. He then turned left down the lane, passing the old station building, and onto the level crossing, one of the new type of automatic open

Left: The level crossing at Lockington, an automatic open crossing remotely monitored (AOCR), at the time of the accident (1986). The symbols at the top of the road traffic signal posts were intended to convey to the road user the fact that this is a railway level crossing with two lines and to make more visual impact. It is now an automatic half-barrier crossing, although it was precisely the type of crossing for which AOCR was designed, being lightly used, mainly by local road traffic. *Stanley Hall*

Left: The driver of the van which caused the collision at Lockington emerged onto the road from the buildings on the left. He had only a short-range view of the flashing red lights but knew the crossing well. *Stanley Hall*

Right: Class 47/4 diesel No 47 627 approaches Third Drove automatic half-barrier crossing (AHB) on 13 June 1987 with a Newcastle–Great Yarmouth express. There are five AHB crossings within the space of two miles on this stretch of line between March and Ely. *Michael J. Collins*

Below: An automatic open crossing locally monitored (AOCL) at Dolau, on the Central Wales line. It has a very sparse train service, but the station is beautifully maintained by the local community and wins many competitions. This photograph was taken in 2003. *Stanley Hall*

level crossing remotely monitored (AOCR) which had been installed only a few months previously. The old gates of the level crossing had gone and they had been replaced by flashing red road-traffic signals operated automatically by approaching trains and easily visible from hundreds of yards up the lane. Unfortunately, the van driver had not approached the crossing from hundreds of yards up the lane, but from only a few yards. He had just a few seconds' view of the road-traffic signals and went past them. They were certainly flashing, as witnesses subsequently testified.

At the precise instant when the van proceeded onto the crossing so did the train. It hit the van squarely in the middle, smashing it to pieces, but part of it got underneath the train, derailing it. The derailed train careered onwards for about 150yd, then the first coach reared up and turned completely round on itself, landing on its side in a field. The other coaches came to rest in a zigzag pattern, leaning over slightly. Eight passengers were killed, and 37 were seriously injured. The train driver was also seriously injured. He was based at Bridlington and had been with BR for 35 years. He never worked again and died four years later. The van driver, who had no recollection of the accident, survived but his passenger, his 11-year-old son, was killed.

The fallibility of automatic open crossings was demonstrated again, but in one way this was a freak accident. The van driver had

Left: Paignton station and its level crossing, with manually-controlled barriers that close the whole road. It is a very busy crossing, both with road vehicles and with pedestrians. This scene was recorded on 12 September 2007. *Stanley Hall*

only a few seconds' view of the road-traffic signals and his need to concentrate was not high because he was making a regular journey on a very quiet road. His attention may have been diverted at the crucial moment by his son or the dog.

Much attention was directed by the succeeding inquiries into the safety of AOCR crossings. If this had been an AOCL crossing the collision would probably still have occurred, but at a lower speed with less severe consequences. Clearly, the risk of user error is greater than at an AOCL crossing, but it is also greater than at an AHB crossing because the barrier is a visual impediment to progress. With hindsight, the AOCR was a design of crossing that was too optimistic when the behaviour of road users, either deliberate or unintentional, was taken into account.

The public inquiry

The public inquiry was held by one of the Inspecting Officers of the Railway Inspectorate, Department of Transport, Major A. G. B. King. There was ample evidence that the flashing road-traffic signals

Left: Class 158 'Express' DMU No 158 855 passes over the level crossing and enters at Paignton station on 12 September 2007 as a crowd of pedestrians wait for the barriers to rise. Those of an impatient or athletic nature may negotiate the 61 steps of the footbridge if they so wish. *Stanley Hall*

Right: Site of the tragedy of 6 November 2004 at Ufton automatic half-barrier level crossing, between Reading and Newbury, photographed on 1 August 2007. The car driver who committed suicide had parked his car near the spot where the taxi is standing and then drove forward onto the crossing when the road-traffic signals began to flash. Nothing appears to have changed here since the accident. *Stanley Hall*

Below left: The approach to Ufton level crossing from the Reading direction. *Stanley Hall*

Below Right: Ufton – the view along the track towards Newbury. The points in the line ahead caused the derailed train to be diverted to the left, making the accident much more severe. *Stanley Hall*

were working properly and Major King came to the only possible conclusion, that the van had been driven past them and onto the crossing. How or why are immaterial. Safety at AOCR crossings depends entirely on the road user, and the railway authorities had handed over that responsibility, relying upon the crossing equipment. In concept, the safe operation of the railway system had always relied upon a well-trained and responsible workforce, properly supervised. That responsibility so far as AOCR crossings were concerned, and indeed at AHB crossings too, had been handed over to millions of road vehicle drivers of varying degrees of responsibility and competence. Not a particularly good exchange, it might be thought, but BR was required by the Government to reduce its financial support and its manpower. And the Department of Transport was anxious to reduce delays to road traffic at level crossings, but wasn't prepared to pay for bridges.

The comments in Major King's report are worth repeating here:

> 'Under certain circumstances some motorists either do not notice the red traffic-light signals flashing or, if they see them, do not comprehend or understand the message that is given by them. This is not wilful disobedience but

the fact that the message given by the signals is inadequate for some.

> 'Some motorists after seeing the red lights flashing, act in a most irresponsible manner at the crossings. This results from stupidity, impatience, or a lack of appreciation of the hazards.

> 'BR has fallen short of what they should do to record and explain unusual occurrences, to deal with safe-side failures, and to encourage reports of such incidents.

> 'I have considered that the most effective way to reinforce the message to motorists that they must stop when the lights flash is to provide some form of barrier.

> 'I have found in the course of my inquiry a most casual and thoughtless attitude among some road users of the crossing.

> 'Improvements are needed in that part of the Highway Code that deals with level crossings.'

Professor Stott's review of automatic open level crossings

Doubts about the suitability of automatic open crossings had been growing within the Railway Inspectorate and BR for some time, and matters were brought to a head by the Lockington accident. The Chief Inspecting Officer of Railways had already decided that no further authorising Orders for automatic open crossings would be made pending an independent review of their safety record, and this decision was announced in Parliament on 28 July 1986. An independent review was necessary because of the involvement of several sections within the Department of Transport as well as within BR. Accordingly, Professor P. F. Stott was appointed to carry out the review. He was assisted as Technical Assessor by Alan Goode, formerly head of the Traffic Engineering Department of the Transport & Road Research Laboratory.

As might be expected, the review produced little that was new, and it did not condemn AOCR crossings entirely, although the Railway Inspectorate had already decided that they would not have any more and that they would require BR to convert the existing 44 AOCR installations to other types of crossing, mainly AHB. This decision had the general support of many within BR. Professor Stott mentioned that BR had planned to install a further 65 AHBs, 105 AOCRs and 52 AOCLs by December 1992, and it was obvious that those plans would have to be considerably amended. Professor Stott's recommendations, thankfully modest in number, finally set the scene for the next 20 years and ushered in a period of much-needed stability.

Left: Hest Bank manually-controlled barrier crossing, near Morecambe, pictured 10 July 2007. Hest Bank is the haunt of holidaymakers and bird-watchers. The busy nature of the line causes the level crossing to be closed to road traffic for quite lengthy periods, hence the footbridge, which replaced an earlier structure. *Stanley Hall*

Left: The very high footbridge at Hest Bank at least provides a grandstand view of trains, birds and coastal scenery. *Stanley Hall*

Above: Elsenham station and manned, gated level crossing, between Bishop's Stortford and Cambridge, photographed on 31 August 2007. A few months earlier this had been the scene of a double pedestrian fatality, which occurred on the foot crossing. *Stanley Hall*

Right: Another view at Elsenham, showing the gated foot crossing with pedestrian warning lights, which have since been replaced by metal gates controlled by the crossing keeper. *Stanley Hall*

This stability can best be demonstrated by a comparison of the number of crossings of each type in 1990 and 2006:

	1990	2006
Manned gates	383	213
Manned barriers	320	238
Barriers with CCTV	275	377
AHB	412	451
ABCL	5	50
AOCL	206	128

Notes:

1 Overall, the total number of public-road protected level crossings has declined from 1,601 to 1,457, an average of nine a year, mainly through closures or replacement by bridges.

2 The number of level crossings operated locally with gates or barriers has declined from 703 to 451, with an increase in remote operation monitored by CCTV of 102.

3 There has been a modest increase of 39 in AHB crossings and a considerable increase of 45 in ABCL crossings.

4 There has also been a sizeable reduction in AOCL crossings, partly as a result of Professor Stott's recommendations. They have mainly been replaced by ABCL or even AHB installations.

5 The total number of automatic crossings has remained almost static.

6 The continuing dependence on non-automatic crossings is a reflection of higher line speeds, and the increasing weight being given to safety, which had a higher profile in 2006 than in 1990.

Left: The new footbridge at Elsenham, allowing pedestrians to cross the line when the vehicle and pedestrian gates are locked. This is not for the faint-hearted — there are 101 steps — and must be one of the most expensive footbridges ever built to cross two lines. *Stanley Hall*

Left: View of the level crossing, new footbridge and London-bound platform at Elsenham. The crossing keeper resides in the grey cabin next to the crossing. *Stanley Hall*

7   ABCL crossings are to all intents and purposes identical to AHB crossings so far as the road user is concerned, but are very similar in operation to AOCL crossings with the addition of a half-barrier which extends across the entrance to the crossing leaving the exit clear. This new arrangement is based on the philosophy that in some circumstances a lowered barrier is more visually arresting than the flashing red road traffic signals.

Safety at public level crossings since 1991

Even though the number of accidents at AHB crossings has been relatively low, they have provided the greatest source of danger. On 8 January 1992 an articulated heavy goods vehicle crashed through the barriers at Dimmocks Cote AHB crossing, near Ely, and was still moving when it was struck by a two-car 'Sprinter' diesel multiple-unit travelling at 70mph. The train was completely derailed but remained almost upright. Of the train's 57 passengers, 42 and the two traincrew required hospital treatment.

Two months later a van carrying two parents and five children zigzagged round the barriers at Fulbourne AHB crossing, between Cambridge and Newmarket, and was struck by a DMU travelling at 60mph. The father and a child were killed and the other five occupants of the van were severely injured. As seen previously, road vehicles with multiple occupancy are often involved in zigzagging accidents.

And there was yet another tragic accident on 4 April 1992 at Thorne Moorends AHB, between Hatfield & Stainforth and Goole, when the driver of a car containing five young people crashed into the side of a DMU, killing himself and two sisters. The remaining two passengers were seriously injured. The driver was under the influence of alcohol. Shortly afterwards there was a near miss at the same crossing, again caused by zig-zagging.

There was almost a replay of the 1968 Hixon accident at Mucking Crossing AHB, near Tilbury, on 2 April 1992, when an abnormal load consisting of a tractor unit hauling a low-loader trailer and carrying a large excavator, with a police escort, went over the crossing without the signalman being contacted, and grounded on the crossing, where it was hit by an electric multiple-unit. Fortunately the train driver had seen the obstruction when 200yd away and was able to reduce the speed of the train to about

35mph. There were no fatalities or serious injuries, but the leading coach was derailed and badly damaged. There was some confusion between the lorry driver and his mate, who tried to phone the signalman for permission to cross, but, having received no reply, went over the crossing to try the telephone at the other side. Unaccountably, the lorry driver took this as an indication that it was safe to cross, and became grounded on the crossing.

What has become a typical type of accident occurred at Funtington AHB crossing (between Bosham and Southbourne stations) on 17 January 1996 just before midnight when a car carrying three men zigzagged round the barriers and was hit by a train. Two of the men were killed and the third seriously injured. This is only the tip of the iceberg, as there are many near misses.

Naworth AHB level crossing, between Haltwhistle and Carlisle, has a melancholy history. Back in 1926 an express passenger train hit a charabanc on the crossing, killing eight of the passengers in the road vehicle and the crossing keeper. Since then it has the local reputation of being haunted, partly due to its secluded location on a minor road in the middle of a dark wood. On 15 November 1995 a woman with a dog was fatally injured on the crossing. It is thought her attention was distracted by her dog. Such distraction, by dogs or small children, is often a cause of accident.

Safety at level crossings had been gradually improving throughout the 1990s with fatalities resulting from collisions between road vehicles and trains on level crossings declining to three or four a year, often owing to the upgrading of crossings perceived to be most at risk. In 1998 there was only one fatality from collisions on level crossings, and this fine record continued in 1999, although the notorious crossing at Hixon was again in the news on 21 March 1999 when a car driver zigzagged round the lowered barriers and was struck by a passenger train. The car was cut in two and the driver fatally injured. As recorded earlier, this crossing has since been closed and replaced by a bridge.

The new century started well. In 2000, there were only two fatalities to occupants of road vehicles, one of which was caused by the blocking back of road traffic in a queue. This occurred at Waterbeach AHB crossing (near Cambridge) on 28 November 2000 when a car entered the crossing with the exit blocked and was struck by a train. The driver was killed.

There was a similar accident at Pooley Green AHB crossing, Egham, on 17 October 2000, when an empty passenger train collided with a bus which was stationary in a queue on the crossing. Fortunately there were no injuries to the bus passengers, as they had rapidly left the bus when they realised their predicament, but there was substantial damaged to the train, which was derailed. The bus was destroyed.

AOCL crossings continued to have the worst accident record of automatic crossings, although fatalities were few owing to the lower speeds of trains over such crossings, coupled with a reduction in the number of AOCL crossings. There were 12 incidents in the year 2000, all of which involved motorists who did not stop at the flashing red road-traffic signals. The value of the half barrier at ABCL crossings is evident. There was one fatality that year at Traethmawr AOCL crossing, near Porthmadog.

In 1995 there was the first confirmed suicide at an AHB level crossing since King's Fernsden in 1986, where a car driver parked the car on an AHB crossing and waited for an oncoming train to smash into it whilst the car driver remained seated. This occurred on 16 September at Pirton AHB level crossing, between Ashchurch and Abbotswood Junction, on the Birmingham–Bristol main line. A local man, aged 23, apparently had a row with his girlfriend and drove on to the crossing, then switched off the engine and the lights and waited to be hit by a train, a Bescot to Newport Transrail freight. The car, a Ford Fiesta, was pushed a considerable distance down the track in the direction of Cheltenham. On 7 April 2003 there was another fatality, a suicide, at Dunhampstead AHB crossing, on the same line eight miles nearer Bromsgrove, the train being a high-speed mail train.

Was this form of committing suicide the beginning of a trend, bearing in mind that there may well have been other suicides in the past in which the Coroner felt unable to record a suicide verdict in the absence of sufficient evidence to support such a verdict? There was a rather unusual fatality at Kirknewton AHB crossing, between Edinburgh and Shotts, on 17 February 2004 when a motorist turned off the crossing onto the railway line and drove down the track towards an approaching train. If it were done accidentally, one might expect a motorist to recognise immediately that he had done so by the roughness of the terrain, then stop his car, get out, and telephone the signalman from the crossing without delay.

The disaster at Ufton AHB crossing

This was similar to the Dunhampstead and other suicides, but with far graver consequences. As so often happens in accidents, the difference between the consequences at Dunhampstead and that at Ufton AHB crossing, between Reading and Newbury, depended on a quite unrelated factor, in this case a pair of facing points beyond the crossing, which turned what might have been a minor derailment into a major disaster.

On Saturday 6 November 2004 the 17.35 HST from Paddington to Plymouth called at Reading then, after negotiating the 40mph curve to Reading West, its speed rapidly increased to just below 100mph, the maximum line speed. The line curves to the right approaching Ufton crossing and it would appear that the driver saw the car on the crossing when he was about 200yd away. He immediately shut off power and moved the brake handle to the Emergency position. The impact derailed the first pair of wheels but the train continued forward, losing speed rapidly over the next five seconds to 64mph when it reached a pair of facing points into the Down Goods Loop, which diverted it to the left and down a shallow embankment. All eight coaches were derailed.

The train driver, Stan Martin, was killed when the power car turned onto its side and an incredible amount of soil and ballast was scooped up as the front of the vehicle dug in, filling the driving cab and burying the driver, who was eventually found in a corner of the driving cab. The train was carrying over 300 passengers and six were killed. Seventeen of the injured were detained in hospital.

According to press reports, an off-duty policeman saw the vehicle on the line at the crossing and thought that it had stalled, but the driver, when the policeman approached him, is said to have told him that he 'just wanted to die'. As the crossing barriers began to close, the policeman ran to the emergency phone but said he could obtain no reply. There would still have been time to reduce the force of the impact if the signaller had been told at once, because there is a signal, R808, only about 200yd before the crossing and it could have been seen by the train driver at red some distance away. The crossing closure sequence takes a minimum of 27 seconds, and at 27 seconds' running time a train approaching at nearly 100mph is about three-quarters of a mile away. The vital action in such circumstances is to tell the signaller immediately and not waste a second.

The causes of an accident are generally known, but the consequences are almost always unknown. That is the importance of considering the potential consequences of an accident rather than the actual consequences. The reaction to the Ufton accident should be no different from any of the other AHB accidents, but it is difficult to resist the enormous pressures, except to the extent that it serves as a wake-up call or indicates a trend. With that caveat in mind, nothing should be done after Ufton that would not have been done before it. That is the accident practitioner's mantra.

After Ufton

There were two fatal collisions at AHB crossings in 2005. At 09.45 on 17 September a 92-year-old car driver was killed when he drove into the side of a train at Rillington AHB crossing, on the York–Scarborough line, and at 13.15 on Sunday, 13 November a car driver was killed on the Swainsthorpe AHB crossing, just south of Norwich, in a collision with a train. The car then caught fire. The line speed is 80mph. A witness waiting at the same side of the crossing is reported to have seen a car drive onto the crossing and position itself directly in the path of the train. Another witness is reported to have seen the car parked on the offside of the road close to the level crossing beforehand. This is precisely what happened at Ufton AHB crossing and tends to suggest strongly that the Swainsthorpe collision was caused by a suicide, which was confirmed by the Coroner's inquest.

Swainsthorpe was again in the news on Thursday, 1 March 2007 when a Norwich-bound train, travelling at about 100mph, struck a car on the crossing and killed the driver. By then the line speed had been increased to 100mph. At the Coroner's inquest it was accepted that there was no fault with the AHB equipment. The coroner directed the jury to return a verdict of Accidental Death.

There was a similar accident a few days earlier, on 23 February at Gailes AHB crossing, between Barassie and Irvine, when an electric multiple-unit running empty, struck a Network Rail van, killing the driver. Suicide was suspected.

Left: The view north at Swainsthorpe automatic half-barrier crossing, five miles south of Norwich on the line to Ipswich and London, and the site of a collision between a train and a car on 13 November 2005. The Coroner's verdict was suicide by the car driver, who parked his car where the white car is standing in this photograph (taken 29 November 2007) before driving onto the line. *Stanley Hall*

Below left: The view north from Swainsthorpe level crossing, 21 September 2007. *Stanley Hall*

Below: There was a second fatality at Swainsthorpe crossing on 1 March 2007, when a car was hit by a 100mph express heading north. The car driver was killed. He lived near the level crossing, just at the foot of the hill. This picture was taken on 29 November 2007. *Stanley Hall*

There was a double pedestrian fatality at Elsenham station, between Bishop's Stortford and Cambridge, on 3 December 2005, when two girls were struck and killed as they crossed the line between the platforms to catch a train standing in the far platform (the platforms are staggered, each one being beyond the gated level crossing). They had failed to obey the miniature warning light at the wicket gate, which was at red. The lights have now been removed, and the wicket gates are controlled by the crossing keeper. A footbridge has also been erected to allow passengers to cross the line when the wicket gates are locked. A further seven pedestrians were struck and killed at crossings in separate incidents during 2005.

For the first time ever, there were no fatalities in 2006 amongst traincrews, passengers or the occupants of road vehicles, at either protected or unprotected (mainly private) crossings, a remarkable record. There were only two pedestrian fatalities at protected crossings, both at AOCLs.

Both Network Rail and HM Railway Inspectorate have introduced policies to improve level-crossing safety, which is now generally regarded as one of the last great unsolved risk areas. Both policies are full of praiseworthy objectives but need positive action. AHBs provide the greatest area of risk and that risk could quickly be reduced if the maximum line speed on which AHBs are allowed was reduced from 100mph to 75mph. That is the single most positive step that could be taken. Education programmes, publicity and lots of talk might reduce zigzagging at AHB crossings, which is the cause of most collisions at AHBs, but zigzaggers are likely to be impervious to reason.

Stronger action is needed and the British Transport Police have erected cameras at some crossings where misuse is most severe. However, the penalties imposed by the courts when offenders are brought before the magistrates are often an insufficient deterrent. Both the British Transport Police and Network Rail have mounted publicity campaigns to bring home the dangers, including dramatic TV shorts illustrating the dangers of ignoring the flashing red lights.

However, Network Rail has had one success. It has persuaded Parliament to include powers in the 2006 Road Safety Act to allow the Department for Transport to issue orders to highways authorities to make road improvements approaching level crossings, such as double white lines, positive lane separation, rumble strips and traffic-calming measures. The ultimate solution is the replacement of level crossings by bridges, but the cost of these varies between £3 million and £4½ million. Costs can be even higher, depending on the local circumstances; the bridge at Tile Hill, between Coventry and Birmingham, cost £6½ million.

Dealing with potential suicides is a greater problem, and can only be mitigated or solved by closing the gap at half-barrier crossings or providing them only on lower-speed lines. The railway industry can apply remedies at public level crossings if it wishes to do so; the problem at private crossings is much more intractable, as we shall see in the next chapter.

However, to keep the matter in perspective, the causes of major accidents in the last 10 years have been as follows:

Cause of accident(s)	Number of accidents	Location(s)
Defective track	3	Hatfield, Potters Bar, Grayrigg
Collision with road vehicle, not at level crossing	1	Great Heck
Signal Passed at Danger	1	Ladbroke Grove
Collision with road vehicle at level crossing	1	Ufton

The accident record of fatalities at public-road level crossings caused by collisions between trains and road vehicles since 2000 is as follows (occupants of road vehicles and trains only):

Year	2000	2001	2002	2003	2004	2005	2006
MG							
MCB							
CCTV							
AHB	1	2	1	2	8	2	
ABCL							
AOCL	1						

(2006: Nil in all categories)

This table shows the preponderance of fatalities at AHB crossings. Train passenger fatalities are uncommon, the collision at Ufton in 2004 being the exception when five train passengers and the train driver were killed. In the last 50 years there have been only two other cases of multiple fatalities among passengers — at Hixon in 1968 and at Lockington in 1986, but train drivers are sometimes

Below and below left: Two photographs provided by Network Rail in 2007 as part of its campaign to improve driver behaviour at level crossings. *Network Rail (both)*

killed when there are no passenger fatalities.

Whether occupants of road vehicles die or not in collisions at level crossings is often purely a matter of chance. Most train/road vehicle collisions occur either at automatic half-barrier crossings or at automatic open crossings. Those at AHBs are potentially the more serious owing to the higher train speeds usually involved. Annual averages over the period 2000 to 2006 for train/road vehicle collisions are in the region of four for all AHBs in total and five for AOCLs.

On 2 February 2007 there was a serious accident at Delny automatic open crossing (locally monitored), between Invergordon and Tain, when three 17-year olds in a car were in a collision with a train on the Wick/Thurso line. Two passengers were killed, but the driver survived and was jailed for five years after admitting dangerous driving. None of the 14 passengers and four staff in the two-car DMU, running from Inverness to Wick, was injured.

Details of accidents in 2008

Level crossing accidents from unusual causes continue to plague the railways. On 4 January 2008 a Class 37 diesel travelling light (i.e. with no train) at 55-60mph hit a lorry carrying potatoes which had become immobilised on Whitemoss AHB crossing, between Gleneagles and Perth. It is thought that snow and ice on the road crossing surface had rendered the lorry unable to move. Unfortunately the lorry driver had failed to use the emergency telephone to warn the signalman. This accident underlines yet again two fundamental problems — the failure of road vehicle drivers to use the emergency telephones, which renders them useless, and the suitability of AHBs for a 90mph line.

Wraysholme public level crossing, between Grange over Sands and Ulverston, used to be a gated crossing worked by a crossing keeper but was converted to an automatic open crossing locally monitored (AOCL). In March 2008 there was a collision between a car and a train in which the car driver was seriously injured. AOCLs do not have a good accident record, but because train speeds are generally lower than at AHB crossings, casualties are likely to be lighter. Train drivers approach such crossings prepared to stop if the crossing is seen to be obstructed, but there is little they can do if a car suddenly appears in front of them when they are almost at the crossing.

Children 'playing around' near level crossings are occasionally killed when they stray on to the railway line. In June 2008 some teenage girls were reported as 'messing around' near the manned barrier level crossing at Pencoed, near Bridgend, South Wales, when a mobile phone was thrown on to the track. A 16-year old girl climbed over the lowered barrier and was hit by an express train. She was killed.

The AHB problem

The small number of fatalities each year does not justify massive expenditure on a national programme of bridge building and the wholesale upgrading of level crossing protection. Nevertheless the arrow of potential catastrophe is aimed fairly and squarely at AHB level crossings on lines above 75mph. They could and perhaps should be upgraded or bridged. For all the other level crossings there is no easy answer.

But the train driver needs to be remembered. He is at the sharp end and deserves better from his employer, who has both a legal and a moral duty to protect him from harm. And the suicides who park their cars on 100mph lines (there have been several in recent years) are a recent and worrying development, especially to the innocent train driver.

As for the big one, the one with multiple deaths among the passengers, there have been three in the last 40 years and it is a practical impossibility to protect all the thousands of crossings, both public and private, against such an event. But the risk can be reduced by not having AHB crossings on lines above 75mph.

To summarise the present situation, the number of public-road level crossings of each type at the end of 2006 was as follows:

Manually-controlled gates	213
Manually-controlled barriers	238
Manually-controlled barriers with CCTV	377
Automatic half barriers	451
Automatic barrier crossing locally monitored	50
Automatic open crossing locally monitored	128

The future

- Network Rail proposes to modernise or replace with bridges about 250 level crossings between 2009 and 2014 at a cost exceeding £200 million. Replacing level crossings by bridges is becoming more of a realistic option, as modern technology is reducing the cost of bridging, whilst the costs of automation or the use of CCTV for monitoring purposes continue to rise.

- There is a relatively new system of achieving a standard arrival time at a crossing based on measuring the speed of an approaching train, with the barriers being lowered at the required moment to achieve the standard arrival time.

- Experiments are taking place on some European railway administrations of monitoring the presence of an obstruction at a full barrier crossing by using radar sweeps instead of CCTV or other remote monitoring. This would avoid the need for visual monitoring of CCTV screens.

- Radar monitoring of obstructions may find an application at AHB crossings, provided means can be found of conveying information to the driver of an approaching train. This could be coupled with the provision of four half barriers to completely close off the road approaches.

- The Law Commission has recently announced that the law governing railway level crossings will form part of its programme of law reform. As this book has shown, most of such law dates from the early days of railways as an obvious development when railways were being built. The Law Commission's initiative is strongly supported by HM Railway Inspectorate (part of the Office of Rail Regulation).

The detailed specifications for each type of level crossing are too voluminous to be detailed in this book, but they can be found in a booklet entitled *Railway Safety Principles and Guidance, Part 2 Section E, Guidance on Level Crossings* originally published by HM Railway Inspectorate in 1996 when it was part of the Health & Safety Executive.

9

DANGER AT PRIVATE LEVEL CROSSINGS

The story of private level crossings in the 19th century was dealt with in Chapter 2, and the years up to 1939 in Chapter 3. This chapter now takes up the story in 1945, at the end of the World War 2. The safe use of a private level crossing continued to be the responsibility of the crossing user, who was required to close the gates behind him. It was (and still is) an offence for a crossing user to omit to shut and fasten any gate after use. All that was required of the railway companies was to act responsibly, and this consisted mainly of instructing drivers to keep a good lookout and sound the engine whistle when necessary. At locations where there was restricted sighting of approaching trains, 'Whistle' boards might be provided. Accidents at private level crossings were quite common, but it was unusual for them to cause serious danger to trains so long as railway engines were bigger and heavier (and faster) than any road vehicle that might use a crossing. But the balance had already been changing in the 1930s as the use of motor lorries became more common, replacing horse-drawn carts, and the likelihood of a serious accident to a train was increasing.

Collision at Connington North, 1 March 1948

This was one of the most serious private level-crossing accidents of all time and it occurred in dense fog at 7.0am at Occupation Crossing No 85, located 80yd north of Connington North signalbox and about eight miles south of Peterborough, on the East Coast main line. There were four lines of way here: the Down Goods, the Down Main, the Up Main and the Up Goods. The crossing had become much busier during and after the war in the interests of food production.

A 2½-ton lorry carrying 11 German prisoners of war from Glatton Camp to work at Glatton and Speechley farms was crossing the line from west to east when it was struck on the Up Main line by a light engine, an 0-6-0, running tender-first at about 20mph. Casualties were heavy; three Germans were killed outright and three more died in hospital. The five others were all seriously injured. An ambulance taking the injured men to hospital collided half a mile from the crossing with a bus travelling

Above right: Besides miniature warning lights the occupation crossing at Harts Drove, near Whittlesea, is provided with five instruction signs and a telephone. However, as suggested by this photograph, taken on 27 September 2007, the arrangement of the signs could perhaps be improved, and the warning lights given greater prominence. *Stanley Hall*

Right: An earlier (1979) photograph of the approach to Harts Drove crossing, showing a neater selection of notices. *Stanley Hall*

Above: The notorious Funtham's Lane occupation crossing, near Whittlesea, pictured on 27 September 2007. At one time this was used by road traffic serving a brickworks, which resulted in several accidents, and in order to secure the safety of the line BR had to apply to the Railway Inspectorate for a Section 124 Order under the terms of the Transport Act 1968; this enabled BR to install lifting barriers and road-traffic signals monitored by CCTV and operated from the nearby King's Dyke signalbox, as though the lane were a public road. *Stanley Hall*

in the opposite direction and bringing railway staff to the nearby marshalling yard. This resulted in a German doctor and a medical orderly being injured.

Later that same year at the same crossing, on 16 October, in rain and failing light, a car travelling from east to west was struck and wrecked by an up empty coaching stock train travelling at 50mph. The car driver was killed.

A typical accident

One of a long catalogue of similar accidents occurred in June 1956 at Walkers Farm Crossing, between Silverdale and Arnside, and demonstrated the inherent dangers of unprotected private crossings. A private car (a 10hp saloon) driven by Mrs Walker, who lived at Waterslack Farm only a few yards from the crossing, was passing over the crossing when it was struck by the 11.45 express from Euston to Workington, travelling at an estimated speed of 40-45mph. She was killed, together with her passenger, her 80-year-old widowed aunt. Members of the traincrew protected the line then ran for help. The fireman went by chance to a house which happened to be Mrs Walker's home, the door being answered by her daughter, who had to be restrained from going to the crossing. The train was undamaged and continued its journey after a short delay, arriving in Workington only 30 minutes late. It was suggested that Mrs Walker knew the times of all the trains, but the express was running a few minutes late.

Some legal changes

After World War 2 the legal position regarding the responsibility for safety at private level crossings began to shift, and a trend emerged of imposing a heavier duty of care upon the railway. The well-known judge, Lord Justice Denning, gave his view in a 1952 case in which he said:

'Apart from statute, the defendants (BR) were under a duty at common law to prevent danger at these crossings. As the danger increases, so must the precautions increase.

The defendants cannot stand by while accidents happen and say, "The increased traffic on the road is no concern of ours". It is their concern. It is their trains which help to cause the accidents and it is often the increased number of trains which increases the danger ... they must do all that may be reasonably required of them in the shape of warning, whistles, and so forth as to reduce the danger to people using the crossing.'

He did not suggest what sort of warnings, nor amplify his 'so forth', but he didn't seem to have anything of a major nature in mind. It was, however, becoming clear that BR could no longer stand back as though it were no problem of theirs at those crossings where road traffic had become heavier and presented a real danger to rail traffic.

Eventually, Section 124 of the 1968 Transport Act gave the Minister of Transport powers to require BR to provide, maintain and operate such lifting barriers, lights, signs or other devices at any level crossing across any road other than a public carriage road. BR could not legally do this without an Order from the Minister, and required this legal device. That enabled them to improve safety at those crossings which had seen increased road traffic to the extent that they began to resemble public road crossings and where something had to be done, especially with the increase in train speeds and the elimination of steam haulage. Diesel and electric trains approached more quietly or were less

Right, below left and right:
An occupation and public footpath crossing at Waterslack, between Silverdale and Arnside, together with instruction and penalty notices. The vehicle crossing appears to be disused in this photograph, taken on 10 July 2007, but in June 1956 was the scene of a double fatality.
Stanley Hall

visible to the crossing user. Those trains were also more vulnerable than a steam engine in the event of a collision.

An accident at Funtham's Lane occupation level crossing, between Peterborough and March, on 27 April 1958, illustrated this problem, which was beginning to be apparent even in steam days. In daylight and fine weather a motor car was being driven over the crossing when it was hit by a steam-hauled passenger train travelling at about 50mph, and wrecked. Its three occupants were all killed. This was a very busy crossing, which led to two brickfields, a farm and some cottages. On an average day it was used by 500 motor vehicles and 400 motor cycles or cycles and the field gates were regularly left open to the road by users of the crossing. Indicators had already been provided which showed 'Train coming — Stop'. Although this was a private crossing at which in law the responsibility for safety belonged to the road user, it was felt that the unsatisfactory situation could not be allowed to continue. The safety of trains was a real danger. Eventually, but not until 1970 and using the powers contained in the 1968 Transport Act, manually-controlled lifting barriers which closed the whole road were installed. They were provided with bells and road-traffic signals and operated from the nearby King's Dyke signalbox, being monitored by CCTV. However, changes in the operation of the brickfields, and in the industrial plant have been made and a new entrance has been made to the site. Funtham's Lane Crossing is no longer busy. But the dangers posed by occupation crossings have not been solved even at the time of writing, 50 years later.

The situation from the mid-1950s

In 1954 there were 21,311 occupation and accommodation crossings and 52 accidents, with 15 deaths and 24 people injured, mainly occupants of road vehicles hit by trains on the crossings. The vehicles involved were two tractors and trailers, three lorries, five motor cars and one motor van. Two freight train engines were derailed.

By 1965 the number of private crossings had been reduced to 14,362, mainly by route closures following the 'Beeching Report'. However, there were 62 accidents, with 12 deaths and 27 people injured. Seven occupants of road vehicles and five pedestrians were killed.

Four years later, with the route closure programme largely complete, the number of private level crossings had declined to 8,837. There were 42 accidents, with 10 deaths and 33 people injured. Five occupants of road vehicles and five pedestrians were killed.

There was a public inquiry into one of the accidents, which occurred at Catholme occupation crossing, Wichnor Junction, between Burton-upon-Trent and Tamworth, at 13.38 on 15 February 1969. A farm tractor towing a trailer loaded with about 2½ tons of manure approached the crossing just as a diesel-hauled coal train was also approaching. The tractor stopped a few feet from the line in the view of the signalman in the Junction signalbox. The signalman put up his hand to warn the tractor driver not to cross. As soon as the coal train had passed over the nearer line to the tractor, the driver set off behind it, having taken the signalman's hand signal to mean it was safe to do so, straight into the path of a diesel multiple-unit coming the other way on the far line. The DMU, travelling at about 60mph, hit the middle of the trailer and was completely derailed, with the leading car upside-down and the two other cars across both lines on their sides. Fortunately, the train was lightly loaded and all 20 passengers were travelling in the rear cars. Eight of them were taken to hospital, but not detained. The unfortunate train driver was more seriously injured, including two broken legs. As was customary in those days, there was no delay in removing the three derailed cars, enabling this important main line to be reopened 20 hours later.

The National Farmers' Union (NFU) had been concerned over the years about the increasing hazards to farm employees at unguarded crossings and, in consultation with the Ministry of Transport, the BRB had recently concluded a detailed examination of all private crossings to assess the problems at each. The BRB then made proposals to the NFU for the sharing of costs to provide additional safeguards, and confirmed that they were ready to make an ex-gratia payment of up to £20,000 a year for the next five years for that purpose, provided that:

- There was a 50% contribution from the farmer or landowner in each case

- There must be some benefit to railway safety.

Replying to a question in Parliament, the Minister announced that the BRB and the NFU were drawing up a work programme for the first year.

Incidentally, the Inspecting Officer who held the inquiry into the Catholme Crossing accident said that the occupation level crossing problem needed to be specially considered in the light of the very high-speed light-weight trains, such as the Advanced Passenger Train, currently being planned.

Three years later, in 1972, when the signalbox had been demolished, there was a further high-speed collision at Catholme Crossing, when the driver of a northbound express, travelling at

Left: A simple farm crossing, possibly of the accommodation type, between Bourne End and Marlow, photographed on 20 July 1978. *John Glover*

Left: An accommodation crossing with footpath rights between Minster and Ramsgate, 17 April 1961. *BR*

Level Crossings

Right, middle and bottom left: An occupation and footpath crossing at Moulinearn, south of Pitlochry, the site of a fatality in 2001 when the miniature warning lights were ignored; a car was hit by an express passenger train, and a passenger in the car was killed. This accident and others of a similar nature sounded warnings that miniature warning lights are not the complete answer to safety at occupation (or pedestrian) crossings. These photographs show respectively the crossing and the view down the line, the approach to the crossing from the main road, and the approach to the crossing and the main road from the hamlet. The barriers are operated electrically, one of the few such instances. *Stanley Hall (all)*

Bottom right: After the accident, certain changes were made, including duplication of the miniature warning lights — a non-standard arrangement. *Stanley Hall*

85mph, saw a tractor and plough suddenly appear from behind the rear of a stationary freight train and cross the line in front of him. He had no time to brake and struck the plough, hurling it aside. The train was not derailed, and was brought to a stand several hundred yards down the line. After examination, the train was allowed to proceed to Derby. A railway officer travelling with the driver walked back to the crossing, but the tractor and driver were nowhere to be found. At a subsequent meeting, the landowner and BR agreed to pay for a bridge on a 50/50 apportionment of the cost, which allowed Catholme and three other adjacent crossings to be closed.

A wake-up call

The progress being made in providing safety equipment at private level crossings, together with the reduction in the number of private crossings which by 1975 stood at about 6,500, is revealed in a reduction in the number of accidents and fatalities at unmanned crossings. There were 28 accidents, but only four

fatalities. However, the following year, 1976, there was a serious collision at Chivers occupation level crossing (No 1) between Lakenheath and Shippea Hill on the Norwich–Ely line.

On 19 December, a six-wheeled Volvo lorry loaded with carrots was crossing the line in thick fog and with darkness falling, after its driver had ignored a conspicuous sign telling him to telephone the signalman to find out if it was safe to cross. At the same moment, a diesel multiple-unit came out of the fog and smashed into the lorry at 50mph. The train driver was killed and several passengers were hurt, but the lorry driver escaped unharmed. The train was not derailed, but the lorry was hurled to one side. However, the accident sounded a warning – the train might come off worse next time by being derailed, resulting in multiple casualties.

There had been a very similar accident at this crossing six years earlier, in December 1970, in thick fog when again the innocent train driver was killed, and it was decided to provide telephones to Shippea Hill Station signalbox. Conspicuous signs were erected next to the telephones with clear instructions to crossing users to telephone the signalman to find out if a train was coming, but there was evidence that crossing users frequently failed to use the telephone. In that respect it was no different from many other crossings where telephones were provided. Failure to use the telephones was endemic. In the month of September 1976 only six telephone calls were recorded in the signalbox at Shippea Hill, whilst in the fortnight following the accident there were 512 calls because the farmer had placed a man at the crossing to supervise its use. The same situation applied to the crossing gates, which should have been closed by each road vehicle user after crossing. They were open on the occasion of the accident, as on many other occasions. This accident illustrated very clearly the radically different approach to safety among drivers of road vehicles compared with railway staff.

The situation obviously couldn't be left as it was. Therefore BR, using its powers under the 1968 Transport Act, erected

Right: The gate leading to Middlebarrow Quarry, Arnside, photographed on 10 July 2007. The quarry is now closed, but at one time it was very busy, with heavy lorries passing over the crossing at frequent intervals and creating a dangerous situation. After many complaints from train drivers the quarry owner placed a gateman at the crossing, whose job it was to telephone the signalman to check if it was safe for the crossing to be used. *Stanley Hall*

flashing red road-traffic signals, and the crossing became to all intents and purposes an AOCL crossing. The lorry driver was tried on charges of manslaughter and endangering the safety of persons on the railway, at Norwich Crown Court. His plea of not guilty to the charge of manslaughter was accepted, but he admitted endangering the safety of persons on the railway and was given six months, suspended for two years, and fined £100. Yet again the courts had failed to take strong action to send the appropriate signals to users of private crossings.

Progress since 1980

In 1980, 1985 and 1990 the number of private level crossings in the various categories was:

	1980	1985	1990
Unmanned with gates or barriers	6,017	5,001	4,529
Unmanned with gates or barriers and telephone	551	698	809
Unmanned with gates or barriers and MWL	45	80	100

(*The figures for MWL crossings for 1985 and 1990 are approximate.*)

A small number of private crossings had been converted to AOCL crossings, and the number of protected private crossings increased by 50% over the 10-year period.

Fatalities at private crossings were as follows:

	1980	1985	1990
Unmanned with gates or barriers	1	3	5
Unmanned with gates or barriers and telephone	0	0	1
Unmanned with gates or barriers and MWL	0	0	0

All five of 1990's fatalities at unmanned crossings without telephones or MWL were pedestrians. In one, a young girl was killed whilst opening the gates; in another a seven-year-old girl ran in front of a train; and in a third a woman was killed whilst chasing her dog. Dogs which escape from control at level crossings are often the cause of human deaths or injury.

The accident at Nairn's accommodation level crossing, 4 May 1982

This level crossing connected fields on one side of the line with fields on the other and was located between Forteviot and Hilton Junction signalboxes on the main line from Stirling to Perth. It was constructed of stone ballast. There were the usual field gates on each side of the line and there were 'STOP, LOOK, LISTEN' boards, which also included instructions to users that they must notify the Station Manager before crossing with a vehicle which was unusually long, wide, heavy or slow moving.

A Ford tractor hauling a 21ft-long low loader trailer carrying a three-piece Cambridge roller weighing about two tons, was being taken across the line when the trailer grounded and became stationary, with the tractor across the Down line. The driver was attempting to move it when he noticed that the gates at Forteviot level crossing were being opened for a train, whereupon he started to run towards Forteviot to warn the signalman.

The train was the 13.35 express passenger train from Glasgow Queen Street to Aberdeen and consisted of seven Mk 2 coaches hauled by a diesel locomotive, No 47522. It was travelling under clear signals at about 90mph when the driver saw the obstruction ahead and immediately made an emergency brake application, reducing speed to about 55mph at the point of impact. The locomotive was derailed to its left-hand side and plunged down the embankment, embedding itself in a lineside dyke, which caused it to pivot round and come to rest on its side, facing the direction from which it had just come. The driver survived the impact and managed to escape from the wreckage of his cab.

The leading coach was thrown across the Up line and came to rest, upright, down the embankment, with its rear end across the Up line. The second and third coaches came to rest on their sides down

Left, below left and below right:
Three views of Bailey's Farm occupation crossing, near Whittlesea, recorded on 27 September 2007 and showing respectively the road approach, the warning notices and telephone, and the surface of the crossing itself.
Stanley Hall

the embankment. The train was carrying about 150 passengers, of whom 30 were taken to hospital, but remarkably only one was seriously injured. The Mk 2 coaches had proved their crash-worthiness and hardly any windows were broken. The accident happened at 14.46 and both lines were reopened 24 hours later.

The accident occurred mainly because the level crossing surface was inadequate for tractors and farm vehicles, and it was found that there were many other level crossings in Scotland in the same condition. Remedial action was taken. Nairn's Crossing had a fair degree of usage and the restricted sighting of northbound trains was obviously a danger. A telephone to the signalman was therefore subsequently provided under the cost-sharing agreement agreed with the National Farmers' Union. This accident, and others before it, seemed to encapsulate the ambivalence which the railway authorities had always had towards private crossings, dating back to the early days of railways, when virtually all responsibility for safety at private crossings was heaped upon the landowner. Lord Denning was right.

Two features of this accident ought not to be allowed to pass unnoticed. One is the life-saving crash-worthiness of Mk 2 coaches, which set the standard for all succeeding builds. The other is the fact that the main line was reopened within 24 hours, which was standard practice for those days, and if it had not been done, heads would have rolled. The present-day railway seems to have lost those skills, and regulatory authorities of various kinds appear to have insufficient concern for the serious inconvenience to many thousands of passengers which extended closures entail.

Into the new century

By the year 2000, telephones had been provided at 1,385 private crossings, whilst 135 user-worked crossings had miniature warning lights. However, there were still 2,425 crossings with no special protection other than gates and notice boards. Only one occupant of a road vehicle was killed that year at a private crossing. That crossing had a telephone to a signalbox.

Considerable progress has been made in closing level crossings, and by 2006 the number of private level crossings with no special protection had more than halved to 1,060. Telephones have been provided at 1,661 crossings. The number of MWL crossings had also declined, either by conversion or closure. That year, no occupants of road vehicles were killed. It might be said that safety at private level crossings was finally being taken seriously by the railway authorities. But it is one thing to provide a telephone; achieving scrupulous use is a different matter. And as experience has shown, even the provision of miniature warning lights does not guarantee that they will be seen and obeyed by the crossing user. Private level crossings continue to be one of the major hazards facing the train operator, as the following recent examples show.

At Pools occupation crossing, between Evesham and Pershore, a new hazard was revealed on 7 July 2003 when the 07.03 express from Hereford to Paddington ran into a minibus conveying agricultural workers. There were no injuries on the train but three passengers in the minibus — one Iraqi, one Indian and one Bangladeshi — were killed. Three others were seriously injured.

Right and below right: Two views of an accommodation crossing just north of Skipton, recorded on 1 October 2007. Note the excellent crossing surface. *Stanley Hall*

The driver of the minibus was a 25-year-old Iraqi asylum-seeker who was unable to read English. The warning signs at the crossing were therefore ineffective and the telephone to the signalman was not used. The use of foreign nationals as agricultural labourers is now widespread, but it is surely a responsibility of their employers to ensure that they are trained in the safe use of private crossings which they need to use during the course of their employment. The driver of the minibus was convicted on three counts of manslaughter and received a five-year jail sentence. He had no driving licence.

There might have been a repeat of this accident on 18 June 2008 when the signalman answered the level crossing telephone and heard a jumble of voices in a foreign tounge. They were evidently trying to cross, but the signalman refused to allow them to do so until he had spoken to their employer. In the meantime he arranged for the drivers of trains to be warned of the circumstances and instructed to approach the crossing cautiously.

In 2005 there were two fatal accidents within a few months of each other at crossings equipped with miniature warning lights. At 18.30 on 30 June a young male driver was killed at Creykes crossing, near Goole, when his car was hit by a diesel unit travelling from Doncaster to Scarborough. Five of the 12 passengers on the train were injured. And at 12.04 on 19 October a tractor driver was killed when crossing the line at Black Horse Drove occupation crossing, near Downham Market. The train was the 10.45 four-car Class 365 electric multiple-unit from King's Cross to King's Lynn, travelling at 90mph.

This chapter has revealed what might be expected – that the majority of accidents occur in the arable lands of the Fen country and East Anglia, where most of private level crossings in regular use are to be found, and often where the tractor or lorry driver is not a regular user of the crossing. The use of these crossings is mainly seasonal, as would be expected. An effective solution to the problem remains to be found.

An effective solution to the problem remains to be found, but the Rail Accident Investigation branch is to carry out an investigation into the risks at user-worked level crossings, after there were seven collisions (and no fewer than 148 reported near misses) at such crossings between June 2006 and November 2007. The study will include a collision between a passenger train and a tractor at Loover Barn crossing near Glynde on 13 June 2008.

However, pedestrians continue to be killed by trains when using footpath rights at occupation level crossings. On 22 January 2008 a young man delivering coal to a house adjacent to West Lodge Occupation crossing, near Haltwhistle, was knocked down by a freight train and killed. The time was 17.13 and it was dark.

On 31 March 2008 an old woman was crossing the line at an occupation crossing near Tackley station on the Oxford to Banbury line, when she was struck by a Cross-Country train. She was on her way to the station.

The theft of signalling cable and metal from railway premises is running at a high level in 2008, but an attempt to steal cable at Lowfield Lane level crossing, between Hull and Brough, was unsuccesful. This was a user-worked level crossing giving access to a cement works, but the works had closed and the crossing was no longer required. The gates were therefore padlocked and the crossing sleepers removed. Footpath rights remained. The thieves cut the padlocks and drove a Sherpa van on to the crossing, but it became stranded across the tracks, where it was hit by a Class 158 diesel unit travelling towards Hull. The train was not derailed, but some windows were broken and one of the 12 passengers suffered minor cuts. The van driver fled from the scene, but it was reported that he was later arrested

DANGER AT FOOTPATH AND BRIDLEWAY CROSSINGS

10

Early developments were dealt with in Chapters 1 and 2, and this chapter takes up the story from 1900.

1900–1960s

There was little change. The railway companies' obligations were to provide gates or stiles and a reasonable surface. After that it was up to crossing users to look out for their own safety. The companies often provided warning notices, such as STOP, LOOK, LISTEN or BEWARE OF TRAINS, and there would probably be a cast-iron trespass notice. Where there was a limited view of approaching trains, a 'Whistle' board might be erected, but in any case a driver would be keeping a good lookout and would whistle in accordance with the Rule if he saw anyone in danger.

These arrangements were generally regarded as adequate as long as train speeds were not high and the trains were hauled by steam engines which generally announced their approach both visually by smoke and steam, and audibly. On electrified lines, however, the crossing user needed to exercise extra care. But despite there being several thousand footpath crossings, only five pedestrians were killed when crossing the line in 1954, the last year before the rapid introduction of diesel multiple-units. Remarkably, in 1957 no pedestrian was killed at a footpath crossing. On the other hand, the railway can be a dangerous place; that year no fewer than 130 trespassers were killed, either walking along the line or taking a short cut across it. On top of that, there were 120 suicides. The combined figure of 250 has remained fairly constant during the last 50 years. In 2006, 181 trespassers were killed and there were 61 suicides, totalling 242. The classification as trespasser or suicide depends on the verdict at the Coroner's inquest. There has always been concern about the number of children under 16 who are killed on the line by trains, but in fact the number is very small by comparison with adults. In 1980 six child trespassers were killed; in 2005 there were five.

Later developments

By 1965 the number of footpath crossings had been reduced to 2,689 owing to route closures, and four pedestrians were killed. By 1970 the number of footpath crossings had decreased still further to 2,174, and four pedestrians were killed. The number of pedestrians killed remained fairly constant throughout the 1970s, but in 1980 the number increased to seven, which included two common causes of accident. In one, a seven-year-old boy was killed by a 'second train' after he had waited for the first train to pass, and in the other a woman was killed when she was taking her dog across the line.

The introduction of High Speed Trains (HSTs) created a new hazard for the users of footpath crossings on those routes, and miniature red/green warning lights were erected at a number of

Left and overleaf: A sequence of photographs, taken in June 1990 at the footpath/bridleway crossing at Carr Lane, south of Doncaster, and showing respectively the entrance/exit gate, the warning notice (with special reference to High Speed Trains), the down East Coast main line (foreground), viewed from the west side, and the crossing, viewed from the east.
Stanley Hall (all)

places. However, their effectiveness depends on the crossing user obeying the red light. In 1985 at Braunstone Footpath Crossing, Leicester, two children were crossing the line after the passage of a train when the red light was still showing, but the light had remained at red because a second train was closely approaching. The elder child crossed safely, but the younger one was struck by the train and killed.

The extent to which children and dogs feature in fatal accidents at footpath crossings was clearly brought out in three of the four fatalities in 1988. At Bailey Lane (LMR) a three-year-old girl ran through the wicket gate ahead of her parents and was struck by a train. At Little Ford (SR) a lady walking her dog was killed. At Car Flatts (ER) a man was struck by a train and killed as he chased his dog. And a man carrying a raised umbrella at Newlands (WR) failed to see an oncoming train.

The following year a girl wearing a personal radio/cassette player was crossing the line to catch a train at Fullers End and failed

to heed the MWL stop light. She was killed. And at Elsenham a lady was killed on the crossing after she also failed to heed the MWL stop light. At Cloven-le-Dale (LMR) a father and a small child he was carrying were both killed by an EMU. A second, older child was uninjured. At Lakenheath a six-year-old child, part of a group, was killed whilst crossing the line behind the train from which they had just alighted. The group was taken unawares by a train closely approaching from the opposite direction.

In 1990 there were still 2,097 level crossings with no form of automatic protection and there were six fatal accidents, including a triple fatality at Carr Lane which attracted considerable media attention. Carr Lane is a footpath and bridleway crossing over the East Coast main line about three miles south of Doncaster. It is a very long crossing consisting of, from west to east, a 70mph bi-directional Slow line, then a wide space followed by the 125mph Down and Up East Coast main line and the 70mph Up Slow line, followed by another wide space leading to the 50mph Up Loversall curve. The crossing mainly connects a nature reserve in the west to a housing estate in the east, and access to the crossing is through self-closing gates.

Above: A Class 156 'Super Sprinter' approaches a crossing near Attenborough, Nottingham, in July 1990. Children play regularly at this crossing, which leads from a housing estate to a nature reserve/leisure area. *Stanley Hall*

Left: Anxious pedestrians watch closely as Class 142 'Pacer' DMU No 142 083 approaches Hirstwood crossing, Saltaire, in July 1990. The crossing lies between a housing estate and a recreational/leisure area.

Right: This well-used crossing leads from a housing area to Otford railway station and is a valuable asset. The line is also well used by third-rail electric trains such as Class 319 No 319 030, seen approaching the crossing on a Thameslink service in July 1990 as a couple of pedestrians wait for it to pass. *Stanley Hall*

At about 7.15pm on 19 June 1990 a woman, accompanied by her two sons and a neighbour's daughter, was attempting to cross the line when she and two of the children were struck and killed by a northbound express, the 17.33 King's Cross to Hull HST travelling at about 120mph. One of her sons, a six-year-old child, was uninjured. According to the train driver they appeared to be crossing from east to west and all of them were wheeling bicycles. The woman was in the lead and the children were spread out over the crossing behind her. When the HST appeared and the driver sounded his horn, the woman threw down her bicycle to the side of the line on which the train was approaching and went back towards two of the children, who were between the two main lines, but the children appeared to be holding on to their bicycles. The woman and the two children then appeared to fall over, and were struck by the train.

Subsequently, consideration was given as to what should be done to make the crossing safer. It is quite safe for two or three adults to cross, taking ordinary care, but danger arises when small children or bicycles, or push-chairs or dogs are being taken, because there is no room for delay in crossing if a train approaches. This is a 125mph line and a train travelling at that speed will cover over 60yd in a second. BR would have liked to close the crossing, but this was resisted by the local council and by the Ramblers Association. A footbridge would cost up to £0.5 million, which at the time no one was prepared to pay. Miniature warning lights would have been very expensive because the controls on five running lines would be extremely complex. In the end, only cosmetic changes were made, until recently. Now a major footpath and bridleway bridge has been erected.

Right: A well-signed and well-maintained footpath crossing at Red Bridge Farm, Silverdale, photographed on 10 July 2007. *Stanley Hall*

The safety record of footpath and bridleway crossings since 1990

Between 1990 and 1999 the average annual number of fatalities at footpath and bridleway crossings was between four and five, a figure which has varied hardly at all for several decades. It is almost as though the irreducible minimum has been reached, bearing in mind that the burden of responsibility for safety at footpath level crossings rests mainly upon the crossing user. The provision of safety equipment at a crossing, such as miniature warning lights, does not remove or transfer that responsibility, and it is surprising that even where miniature warning lights have been provided they have occasionally been ignored with fatal consequences.

In 2008 a 66-year old was knocked down and killed by an electric train whilst crossing the line at Moor Lane footpath crossing, between Staines and Wraysbury, on 16 April. She was a regular user of the crossing and was walking her dog when her foot appeared to have become trapped on the crossing.

Several interesting points have emerged in this chapter, some of which have been mentioned earlier. Some of the fatalities at footpath crossings were recorded by the Coroner as suicides (and excluded from the averages mentioned), but in some other cases open verdicts were recorded which may have been suicides but there was insufficient evidence to return such a verdict. The involvement of bicycles and dogs was surprisingly often a factor in an accident, and sometimes there were suspicions of alcohol. Being killed after crossing behind one train and then being hit by one coming the other way was another recurring factor. The number of elderly people killed was surprising. Some of them were deaf, which would be an additional hazard.

Finally, in 2006 there were still 2,586 footpath crossings and there were two fatalities.

Left and below left: Footpath near Eastrea, Whittlesea, leading to nowhere but a bramble patch and a ploughed field, photographed on 10 July 2007. *Stanley Hall (both)*

AN INTERNATIONAL PERSPECTIVE

11

In the limited space available it is impossible to give an overview of level crossing problems in those interesting faraway places where packed trains, often with passengers hanging from the sides and sitting on the roof, appear to traverse busy local market places and everyone actually survives the experience. A nation like Vietnam, for instance, has a major safety problem: the populace put in level crossings overnight. No one can tell how many level crossings there are, and accidents happen on them. How does one relate that to safety as we define it?

The author has attempted to concentrate on those national networks where research into causes, and mitigating action against, accidents on level crossings pays dividend. Reading the interesting UN ESCAP report it isn't surprising that Australia, Belgium, Canada, France, Germany, Japan, the Netherlands, the UK and the USA are mentioned as the places where level-crossing safety is studied. Those nations have the incentive and the scientific, organisational and financial resources to work on solving problems they experience as intolerable. Public prosperity and development of general safety awareness are inextricably linked and in the less economically developed nations there are more basic survival problems to occupy the mind. Nevertheless, it is pleasing to read that level crossing problems there are being tackled as well, often supported with know-how and financial aid from, amongst others, the nations listed above.

Terminology

The following terminology has been used:
• Road users are level crossing users not travelling on railway equipment and therefore responsible for their own safety. This term comprises everything from pedestrians to the heaviest road vehicles as well as light rail vehicles (trams) not using the intersecting heavy rail line.
• The Open Crossing may have roadside stop signs and Crossbucks or St Andrew's Crosses; a situation known as Passive Protection. It is the responsibility of the road user to stop and look out for trains. Open crossings may have gates that the road user must open and close.
• In Britain there may be train-operated automatic miniature stoplights (MSL), a development not seen outside the UK in Europe. This is a first stage of what is called Active Protection.
• The Automatic Open Crossing or AOC. Like other types of automatic crossing the AOC in Europe is subject to agreements with regard to safe failure modes, road signage (Geneva 1955 & Vienna 1968), layout, presentation of its location and its warning to road users (UIC leaflets 760, 761 & 762). It will be equipped with St. Andrew's crosses, one or two flashing red warning lights and optional bells or warblers activated by an approaching train. Many networks additionally fit a single white flashing light to indicate to the road user that the crossing equipment is in working order and that no train is approaching. In many European nations AOC's are presently being converted into AHB's.
• The Automatic Half Barrier or AHB level crossing has

everything that the AOC has bar the flashing white light, but two half-barrier booms have been added that automatically close when an approaching train is detected. First warning stage yellow flashing lights are added in some nations.
• The Automatic Double Barriers or ADB installation is equipped with two extra half-barrier booms at the exit side for road users.
• The Manual (MFB) or Automatic Full Barrier (AFB) crossing has two crossing barrier booms of sufficient length to close off the entire roadway, often fitted with folding Skirts under them. In most nations the full barrier is allowed for manually operated crossings with direct supervision only to ensure that no road user gets caught between them.

Below: A diesel-hauled Austrian local approaches the open crossing at Pressegger See halt, with St Andrew's cross at the end of the platform. *Peter van der Mark*

Left: An automatic open crossing in the Rockies of Western Canada, very typical equipment for the whole of the Americas and many other places in the world. The installation is being tested. *Peter van der Mark*

Below: An AHB with a difference in Switzerland: this installation allows a narrow gauge train to negotiate a rail/road bridge across a river without road users being present on the bridge. Note the entirely different design of the road traffic signals.
Archive Wim Coenraad

• Manually operated level crossings are being closed through an action from a controlling Crossing Keeper or Signaller, by physically pushing the gates, working levers or wheels or activating power operated crossing equipment. Manual level crossings may be subject to Direct Observation or fitted with Closed Circuit Television (CCTV) and be remotely operated. This way one crossing keeper or signaller may control several level crossings, which considerably reduces the operating cost. A form of manual remote control in France is by radio from the cab of an approaching train.

• Alternatives to barrier booms are horizontally swinging crossing gates or trolley gates rolling in from the sides of the roadway.

Left: A classic Dutch automatic half-barrier level crossing near Ede, on the line from Arnhem to Utrecht. Its US heritage is unmistakable.
Peter van der Mark

Right: The first stage of closing an ADB in St Aignan on the line from Tours to Vierzon in France, where in line with normal European practice first the entry and then the exit barriers close. Note the single flashing red light, also used in Germany .*Peter van der Mark*

Below: An full-barrier installation near Orreklapp, in southern Sweden. *Peter van der Mark*

The safety background

The railways in the world, certainly in the developed nations, are the safest means of mechanised transport available to mankind. The basis of this situation is adherence to safety as the first consideration in operation and strict monitoring of the safety critical operatives.

Level crossings, the function of which is to regulate the crossing priorities of rail and road traffic, are the place where two very different transport cultures meet: the homogeneous, disciplined, professional and safety-first orientated railway culture versus the heterogeneous, largely non-professional and comparatively undisciplined road traffic culture. Whilst to the road user the accident risk on level crossings is not much different from that as is usual on for instance road intersections, to the rail operator it is a serious risk to train safety, and a considerable inconvenience to operations is imported onto the rail system.

The railway operator has little control over what road users do on level crossings and managing that situation with a degree of success is the crux of level-crossing safety. It demands commitment and, unfortunately, serious investment.

Faculties such as character, aptitude, eyesight and hearing in private vehicle drivers are barely looked into in comparison to those of professional vehicle operators. Knowledge of rules and regulations in the majority of road users is proven to be scant, the wish to adhere to them questionable (people deeply dislike to be stopped) and this knowledge and road skills are not re-examined regularly, as is the case with professional operators. They may indeed lose a well-paid specialist job if they fail.

This problem indeed touches the viability of the shared responsibility for safety on the level crossings, as many a motorist's driving attitude differs considerably from the same person in the office or at home. Rational behaviour to travel as risk-free as possible may be freely overruled by emotions of fear, lust, competition and sheer aggression.

Above: A sign along the track at Chemozac, France, that the driver of this train must use the horn (*siffler*, a whistleboard) and use his radio equipment to close level crossing 30bis, 800m from this point.
Peter van der Mark

That does not mention the possible influence of alcohol and drugs on the person behind the steering wheel, the widespread overestimation of staying power against fatigue and the consequences from sheer lack of an innate talent in many to drive a car in a responsible, safe manner. There isn't a country in the world where these issues form part of a selection and monitoring process to allow people to become a private vehicle driver.

This partially explains the sometimes baffling failure by road users to react properly – or at all – to the level-crossing warning indications. Until all motorised road vehicles, like rail vehicles, have a trip data recorder ('black box') displaying incontrovertible facts about the way the vehicle was driven, there is little useful evidence with regard to what the driver's responsibility was in the

Below: An ancient set of trolley gates in the Railway Museum at Utrecht.
Peter van der Mark

run-up to accidents. This lack of exposure to scrutiny frustrates most efforts to achieve safer road user behaviour.

For these reasons road safety, when compared with rail safety, is low. This is aggravated by the fact that there is no well-defined general standard of 'good' driving to fall back on; road vehicle drivers apply their individual ideas about appropriate road behaviour and can't be held responsible for inept behaviour on those grounds.

As a result, the number of fatalities and casualties on the roads is high when looking at the international figures. In 2004 the World Health Organisation in co-operation with the World Bank published a report called: 'Road Safety Is No Accident', which stated that road crashes are the second leading cause of death worldwide among the five to 29-year-olds and the third leading cause of death among the 30 to 44-year-olds. In the same year the UK-based Norwich Union Insurance Group published a road crash index, which showed that whilst 93% of British drivers claimed to be very confident behind the steering wheel of a car (no doubt a figure that is much the same elsewhere in the world) three-quarters of these drivers had been involved in an accident.

It should be borne in mind, though, that level crossing accidents are not at the top of the road or rail traffic accident statistics of any nation. It is only now, when in many European nations railway signalling has been extended with warning and intervention systems to stop train drivers from overspeeding and going through red signals and so virtually eliminated collisions with other trains, that level crossing accidents have taken the pole position on the list of issues to tackle by governments and rail operators. The figures hide the fact that a level crossing incident, like other rail incidents, actually is a fairly rare event. The percentages tend to get inflated out of proportion by one single accident when there are many people involved or the damage is great.

A short history post-World War 2

Up to now, this book has dealt with developments surrounding level crossings in Britain. This did not come about in a vacuum; there were many parallels elsewhere in the world. The introduction of the automatic level crossings in Britain, for instance, proceeded only after a study of examples and their methods of operation elsewhere in Europe.

In 1903, the famous signalling manufacturers Siemens & Halske successfully installed automatic warning lights on the single line from Neuhaus to Senne. Three years later in 1906, the equally famous Swiss manufacturer Oerlikon tested an AHB installation on the electrified Montreux–Oberland Bernois line. Series produced installations could be found throughout Europe and North America from the 1920s onwards.

The aftermath of World War 2 brought the rapid spread of automatic level crossings in Continental Europe. The British railway network came through that period worn out yet intact and fully operational, but most Continental networks had to be rebuilt after the looting and destruction wrought by the occupying armies, resistance movements and the liberation effort of the Allied forces.

The whole presented a unique chance to comprehensively replace lost equipment with up-to-date traction, track, signalling and auxiliary safety equipment such as automatic level crossings, using already existing electro-magnetic relay control technologies that had reached maturity in the USA during the war. Their influence on development in postwar Europe was profound.

The attractions of this hardware were its availability, reliability and ease of maintenance, speed of operation and the potential to save substantially on operations and staff costs. In many cases, it was purchased partially through Marshall Aid, as the domestic industries had often been destroyed.

British differences

Whilst in Britain these new systems would have had to be fitted into the network by replacing existing equipment and altering methods of operation, on the Continent they were an integral part of the reconstruction of the railway. Operating staff were hard to come by and there was no time for training during the Continent-wide rebuilding frenzy after 1945. Circumstances thus favoured automatic operation wherever possible.

Quite typically for the period, the Netherlands thoroughly renewed its railway operations after finding two-thirds of its prewar assets stolen or destroyed. By the end of 1957 steam traction was abolished, relay-controlled multiple-aspect colour lights became the norm for signalling renewals from 1946 onwards, and the AHB level crossing replaced manned level

Right: Trackside manual crossing equipment to be worked by the traincrew at Chemozac, France.
Peter van der Mark

crossings in the newly resignalled sections of the network. This commenced in 1952, the first being Blauwkapel level crossing, just north of Utrecht. By 1963, there were 229 AHB and 425 AOC level crossings in operation.

In 2007 there were 2,800 level crossings left on the network, about one crossing per kilometre of railway line, of which 1,533 were AHBs, five were manned level crossings and two ex-AHBs had become test beds for ADB equipment with radar obstacle detection. All the former AOCs had been converted to AHBs, which reduced accidents to only four level crossing collisions with 11 killed in 2006.

Other European nations show very similar developments. The first (series manufactured) AHB was operational in West Germany in 1951 and in East Germany in 1953. As already recorded, Britain installed the first AHB in 1961. France started in 1954/55, and by 1997 there were 10,800 installations. From the 1950s onwards, Italy and the Scandinavian nations, with their many remote inland railway lines, widely embraced the automatically-operated level crossing during resignalling.

North America

It was the USA where the installation of automatic level-crossing equipment first took off on a large scale in the 1920s. The railroad companies then stopped such installations, as the number of accidents and the consequent damage remained at the same high level that it was before. Incident reporting, however, was often delayed as for a number of reasons the traincrew involved were unable to get information through to the emergency services. The railroad companies opted to keep busy crossings manually secured, preferably with barriers, as the crossing keeper could warn an approaching train or the emergency services, whilst the heavy steel barriers of the period appeared to stop many from foolish initiatives. The steadily rising cost of providing staff, however, especially in remote places, made the AOC and AHB level crossings ever more attractive on financial grounds.

Inevitably, safety suffered. In 1960, 1,421 people died in road and rail vehicles as a result of level crossing accidents throughout the USA. In 1981 (far more cars, far fewer passenger trains, and after a lot of research on level crossing safety) there were still 697 fatalities and 3,121 injured nationwide. In 1998, on 158,719 public level crossings and 100,716 private level crossings, 431 people were killed.

Between 1988 and 1998, Federal Railroad Agency measures such as prescribing that all leading vehicles of a train should be equipped with flashing warning and headlights, reduced level crossing collisions by 18%. This was achieved despite a growth of 15% in rail traffic and 20 million newly licensed motorists flooding the roads. Yet, from a 2007 report, it seems that a Florida to New York passenger train hit cars in two separate level-crossings accidents during a single journey.

A US motorist is 40 times more likely to die on a level crossing than in a collision with another road vehicle. In 1997 a road vehicle and a train collided every one and a half hours on average, which in 1998 improved to every 1hr 58 minutes. Interestingly, 73% of the US level-crossing accidents take place in only 14 states: Alabama, Arkansas, California, Georgia, Illinois, Indiana, Louisiana, Michigan, Minnesota, Mississippi, North Carolina, Oklahoma, Texas and Wisconsin.

In about 75% of the accidents on automatically secured public level crossings in the USA, the blame clearly fell on the road user. This is low in comparison to Europe where the same figure hovers between 85% and 95%, but this disparity might be due to

Above: An AOC of the very first postwar generation spanning four electrified tracks, somewhere in the Netherlands. Such equipment is no longer in use, having been replaced by automatic half barriers. *Archive Wim Coenraad*

different interpretations of the responsibilities of either of the level crossing users, especially when the rail operator is also the owner of the crossing.

Road freight

Worrying the US Government from the 1960s onwards was the rapid increase in high damage collisions between road freight vehicles and trains. It was found that time-stressed truckers endeavoured to cross in front of the slowly approaching and often long freight trains, because these would keep them stopped too long. This is quite understandable when watching a seemingly interminable American freight train trundle across the Main Street level crossing of a small town. The increasingly rare, faster-moving passenger trains (as well as some higher-speed freights conveying perishables, for instance), caught out the offending truckers.

Truckers argued that they noticed the high speed of the train late and then had to decide whether to make an emergency stop and risk jack-knifing their vehicle (which might be a tractor vehicle with two articulated trailers instead of one) or to try and get across in time. As an aside, such safety-related objections do not seem to have surfaced during discussions surrounding the introduction of larger road freight vehicles in Europe.

In the second half of the 1960s this led to the installation of a new division of the US Governmental Department of Transportation, the Motor Carrier Investigation Unit. These are among the cases with which they had to deal.

On 1 March 1960 a Santa Fe passenger train hit a road tank vehicle with 6,465 gallons (approximately 29,000 litres) of oil at Rosedale in California. The fast moving train derailed virtually

Above: A classic ADB installation in the USA. *Milepost 92½*

entirely and the cargo of the tank vehicle ignited. Fourteen people were left dead.

On 17 September 1963 a makeshift bus with 58 Mexican migrant workers was hit by a fast Southern Pacific freight at Chualar, California. Thirty two of the farm workers died and the rest were very severely injured as the light bus-body was ripped from the truck chassis and plastered around the nose of the front locomotive, dropping the bus passengers enmasse onto the track under the moving train.

A Chicago, Burlington & Quincy passenger train hit a dump truck with 30,000lbs (approx 13 tonnes) of aggregates on an automatic crossing near Island Park, Iowa. The truck driver survived and reported that he hadn't seen the train.

Reports of the National Transportation Safety Board (NTSB) in Washington DC contain details of more recent level crossing accidents:

Fox River

In 1996 there was the notorious Fox River Grove crash between a school bus and a commuter train from Chicago. The bus had to stop just after the level crossing for a traffic-light-controlled road intersection and did not clear the tracks by about a metre. The AHB boom came down on the roof of the bus and snapped off, the children initially making a joke of it. They then started to yell and scream in terror at the driver, when they spotted the approaching train sounding its horns. By the time she realised what was happening, it was too late. The train hit the bus at about 30mph (45km/h) while braking in emergency, again separating the bus body from the chassis. Of the 34 children on board, five died instantly and two succumbed later to their injuries.

The root cause was that the bus driver overlooked the length

of the vehicle she was driving. She failed to ascertain that she could clear the level crossing before entering, which world-wide is one of the classic level-crossing accident causes. A contributory cause was that the traffic lights of the intersection and the level crossing installation had not been properly interlinked. Thus they did not allow traffic at the road intersection to clear the crossing when the AHB installation was activated.

As to the late reaction to the screams of the children, the bus had been fitted with sound-deadening upholstery and lining in the roof to stop the noise from the children becoming a distraction to irritable drivers. The third problem was that the driver was a manager standing in for someone who had reported sick. All the regular drivers were aware of the risk at that location but had not passed it on to management. The fourth cause was that the driver had the radio on, which for too long had prevented her from hearing the children and picking up the blaring horn of the approaching train.

On the NTSB recommendation a sign was erected instructing traffic not to enter the level crossing unless the traffic light at the far side allowed exit onto the intersection, so that the level crossing could be fully cleared. As an ironic side issue, the local chief of police and the municipal traffic commissioner were in a car parked near the level crossing, because they wanted to check up on its functioning following a string of previously reported incidents.

On 5 February 1997 in Jacksonville, Florida, the Amtrak 'Silver Meteor' passenger train hit a single articulated road freight combination. This derailed the locomotive and the first four coaches, the locomotive and the first luggage car ending up on their sides with the passenger cars remaining upright. As the trucker saw the accident coming, he jumped off his vehicle and survived the accident without injuries. No one on the train was killed. The truck driver had attempted to use the level crossing to help turn his vehicle, something that occurs in many other parts of the world unbelievable as it may seem. As a result, his driving wheels had rolled off the crossing surface and he lost traction. The trucker had the telecommunications equipment on board to put out a warning about the situation but failed to do so.

The following was a complex accident. It happened on a double level crossing at Portage, Indiana, on 18 June 1998. This location has a single-track freight line and a double-track passenger line, both with their own AHB equipment for crossing the same road, but working independently of each other. The crossings were some distance apart, but not far enough to accommodate a double articulated tractor with two trailers.

This road freight combination, loaded with three steel coils of 19 US tons apiece and secured with a single chain each, stopped for the freight line crossing and fouled the passenger line crossing. A Northern Indiana Commuter Transportation District 2-car diesel passenger train, at some speed and overtaking the freight train, hit the second trailer. The chain securing its 19-ton steel coil snapped, allowing the coil to break away and enter the passenger train by smashing through the driving cab into the passenger compartment. Three people on board were killed.

The level crossing had been under observation already for this particular hazard by Federal, State and private agencies, but action to resolve the issue had not been forthcoming.

On 25 March 1999 the 14-coach Amtrak passenger express *City of New Orleans*, running at 80mph (approximately 130km/h), hit an articulated truck with about 80,000lb (38 tonnes) of concrete reinforcing steel rod on an automatic half-barrier level crossing at Bourbonnais, Illinois, 50 miles (approximately 80km) south of Chicago. That crossing, incidentally, was fitted with constant warning time or 'Predictor' equipment to cut the road traffic waiting time.

The two locomotives derailed and smashed into two out of ten stabled rail freight vehicles in a siding parallel to the main line, coming to a violent stop approximately 50m south of the crossing. The result, was a zigzag pile-up, made worse as it started a fire. Eleven people died and 116 were injured. In the inquiry, it was made clear that due to the many rail sidings the road users experienced frequent long stops as a result of marshalling activities across the crossing. At the same time, local industries resulted in the use of the crossing by at least a thousand road freight vehicles a day.

The train driver and a number of witnesses stated that the crossing had worked as it should, which was backed up with tests. The truck driver, who survived, was one of the many who claimed he had not seen the speed of the train until he was virtually on the crossing and had to decide to brake heavily and risk jack-knifing, see his load come forward and crush his cab, or try and clear the crossing. He turned out to have had a long day driving behind him and to be on a probationary driving licence due to a string of recent speeding offences. The profile was that of a consummate risk-taker.

Australia and New Zealand

There are approximately 9400 public level crossings in Australia, of which 30% has active protection, 64% passive protection and 6% 'other' protection. Several sources indicate that the accident rate at Australian AOC's and AHB's is higher then at passively protected open crossings. This initially looks out of synch with experiences elsewhere in the world, until one discovers that Australia's safety record is actually rather dependent on the scarcity of its rail and road traffic. Accidents at level crossings with active protection, which are mainly found in the comparatively few and far between urbanised areas, occur more frequently because of the

higher frequency of trains and notably road traffic passing the crossing. The main problem in such urban areas is that of private vehicle drivers trying to beat the train to the crossing, in many cases under the influence of drugs or alcohol. The rural area's, where most crossings are passively protected, have very infrequent train traffic whilst road traffic in these same parts is very thin as well, certainly in comparison to eg Europe and parts of North America. The relative chance of a fateful level crossing meet in Australia's vast rural areas is therefore low.

Australia also has a level crossing problem with a nation-specific road freight speciality called the Road Train. Such a road train consists of a tractor vehicle (called the prime mover locally) hauling up to four trailers, the maximum combination known as a B+2A and may weigh op to 120 tonnes.

Consider a typical Australian rural two-lane highway with a permitted road speed of 100km/h (60 mph), crossing a railway line with a line speed of 100km/h or more at an open crossing or an AOC. Not unlike a railway train, under certain circumstances the driver of a B+2A road train combination requires up to a kilometre to come to a controlled stop from that speed. He doesn't, however, always have the advantage of distant signals to indicate the approaching stop point like a railway driver has and it takes therefore little imagination to find fundamentally unsafe conditions here. Especially in the case of e.g. inhibited sighting lines, fog or blinding sunlight do human error and bad luck have a fair chance to wreak maximum havoc.

Another problem with such road trains, indicated in an ATSB accident report from December 2006, is that a trucker with a loaded B+2A road train requires 71 seconds (one minute and 11 seconds) to clear a level crossing after the obligatory stop. In the case of bad sighting lines or fog, this could well mean that a collision with a train doing 120km/h or 75mph is unavoidable as that train will have covered one and a quarter kilometre in that time, with neither driver being able to avoid the looming impact. Such an accident wouldn't take breaching any rules or the presence of any ill intentions. The described problems with unruly urban drivers and road trains received attention in the 2003/04 and 2005/06 National Road Safety Plans of the Australian Transport Council but haven't led to much substantial improvement as yet, mainly due to lack of investment. Moreover, as far as level crossing accidents are concerned, government officials and with them the media have a tendency to flatly blame road users for 'trying to beat the train at the crossing' as the sole source of the problems, which does look like an attempt to avoid having to address the other part of the issue at stake and invest pro-actively in more safety at the many open crossings along heavy freight routes. To convert all remaining public open crossings throughout Australia a sum of Aus $1.5 billion has been mentioned in 2007.

An Australian accident that poignantly illustrates some of the issues mentioned above occurred on the 5 June 2007 at 13:40 AEST along the Murray Valley Highway AOC at Kerang in the Northwest of the state of Victoria.

The sequence started when truck driver Christiaan Scholl, a man with a reputation of being conscientious as well as experienced in driving heavy freight vehicles (three years in Europe and 20 years in Australia), commenced his routine weekly round trip from Wangaratta to Adelaide half an hour late due to late delivery of part of his consignment by the shipper. Driving a prime mover with single trailer combination, he had just returned from a few weeks' holidays, which, incidentally, was identified as a potential contributory issue to railway incidents in the UK some time ago. His delay, moreover, might have influenced his driving

Left: Road freight equipment unknown as yet in Europe, the double-articulated truck. This self-discharging vehicle for bulk transport was photographed at a truck stop somewhere in the Canadian Rockies. *Peter van der Mark*

style as many accidents happened when rail and road drivers were keen on recovery of especially fairly minor delays.

He approached the Kerang AOC at permitted road speed of 100km/h (60mph) from a long, dead straight into a lazy right hand curve that leads up to the crossing and he did notice stationary cars at the other side of the tracks. But, due to misalignment of the warning-light beams and the road glare caused by the strong early midday sunlight, he failed to pick up the warning lights of the AOC whilst the approaching train remained hidden behind a clump of trees. And so, turning the right hand curve on to the approximately 40 degree crossing at an estimated 100km/h (60mph), he suddenly noticed both the flashing warning lights and the train quickly approaching on his left (the locomotive trip recorder revealed that the train was doing about 90km/h or 55mph). By then he had 106 metres (approx 350ft) left to the level crossing and clearly would be unable to stop in time.

Whilst skidding due to heavy braking his truck swerved to the left off the road and impacted with the middle coach of the three-coach locomotive-hauled train. Notably the front of the trailer ripped open virtually the entire side of the coach, derailed it and the combination finally came to a stop more or less parallel to the train facing its direction of travel. With the train still moving, however, the protruding front right corner of the trailer then was hit by the headstock of the rear coach, the impact of which broke its coupler shank and separated it from the train. The trailer then ripped that coach partially open, derailed its front bogie and finally brought it to a stand just past the level crossing. Both impacted coaches of the train remained upright and more or less in line with the track. Eleven passengers died and 23 were injured out of the 40 people on the train.

Given the seriousness of the accident, the Governmental damage limitation exercise kicked in without delay. Later in the afternoon of the day of the accident transport minister Lynne Kosky accused the truck driver of trying to beat the train. This was more forcefully repeated by Victoria police assistant commissioner Noel Ashby, who, during a press conference, dismissed the potential extra safety of half barrier booms as: 'We could have had the Great Wall of China in front of the intersection there and I don't believe it would have prevented this crash. It comes down to driver responsibility'. Two days later, at his hospital bed, Mr Scholl

was formally charged with the blame for the accident, well before the Office of the Chief Investigator had published their investigation report on the accident.

The open official bias unfortunately resulted in Mr. Scholl declining to co-operate with the OCI accident investigation (possibly after misguided union advice) based on lack of trust in its objectivity. He eventually was charged with the full responsibility for culpable driving and indeed, no-one denies that he carries heavy responsibility for the crash due to his irresponsibly fast approach in what he did notice as confusing circumstances at the crossing ahead.

The final chapter in the Kerang level crossing drama, however, is that the AOC subsequently was changed into an AHB and re-equipped with more conspicuous LED warning lights, that were additionally refocused to take the curve in the road in account. Moreover, and crucially important for the heavy freight traffic along this route; asphalt 'rumble' strips and automated distant warning signals have also been provided. Some would interpret that as an implicit admission that the situation at the level crossing perhaps wasn't as safe in all circumstances and free from all blame as some government officials intimated it was.

A year later this same area was again in the news with open crossing incidents when another V/Line passenger train hit a car on the Swan Hill line at Dingee, 70 kilometres North of Bendigo, whilst four weeks later an infrastructure engineering train hit a car at Mitiamo 20 kilometres further along the same line, smashing the road vehicle in two. In both cases the motorists were the only victims.

On the 14 May 2007 the Australasian Railway Association issued a press release mentioning a high-speed crash on a level crossing at Gerogery NSW on 27 January 2001 at 16.07, which criticised the lenient Australian fine culture. It pointed out that in New South Wales a reckless driver could face an AUS $2,200. – fine, but someone not stopping as obligatory at a passively protected open crossing only AUS $308. In fact, apparent irresponsible judicial leniency toward motorists who misbehaved at level crossings is a worldwide source of dismay amongst railway people, many of who can give striking examples. The difficult level crossing at Gerogery, where there was a road intersection near the road/rail intersection which in turn ran like a sort of dog-leg, has been replaced by an overbridge.

The State Government of Victoria later announced a scheme to curb road vehicle drivers from attempting to beat trains at level crossings. Victoria State police criticised the culture of high-risk behaviour in some motorists and proposed creating an offence of speeding to beat the train at the level crossing. Funds to install red light cameras and more active protection are being looked for and

GPS route finding technology might be used to warn motorists that they approach a level crossing. Radar signals using the equipment that many motorists have in their vehicle to detect signals from a speed check radar might be employed. Furthermore raised strip noise paving (rumble strips) will be installed at 200 level crossings. This accident, incidentally, followed 50 previous accidents in the past two years at level crossings in Victoria alone, the Kerang crash was the third fatal accident in the state of Victoria in just over a year. Publication of the National Railway Level Crossing Safety Strategy by the Australian Transport Council was important as an expression of increasing awareness of the problems but as yet still did not lead to more robust action on the subject.

Mr Scholl's case was not helped by the moment in time when he was involved in the Kerang crash. Increased popular awareness of the scale and danger of Australia's level crossing problems was just coming to a head following media coverage after passenger train 'The Ghan' smashed into a road train (without loss of life) at Ban Ban Springs near Darwin, Northern Territory on 12 December 2006, at an open crossing without active protection. In this case the truck driver related how he had used that level crossing many times a day for more then four weeks and only saw four trains in all that time. He had simply got used to rumbling across without stopping or looking out for trains, while safety wasn't served by the fact that he had hearing difficulties and probably missed the sound of the train horns.

New Zealand

In New Zealand the correlation between urban land use, road and rail traffic density and level crossing accidents is also noted in a press release of the 20 July 2008, as 40% of the level crossing accidents over the past five years were in or South of Christchurch and 15 % South of Dunedin. This represents the nation's most densely populated areas and the rail network between Christchurch and Invercargill has 37% of the nation's level crossings. In the North Tauranga City, New Plymouth and Carterton District stood out for the same reasons. Thirteen percent of the accidents took place at barrier-protected level crossings, typically provided at more heavily used level crossing sites in urban areas. Interestingly, fitting barriers costs NZ $150,000.

In the aforementioned five years from 2003 till 2008 there were 149 level crossing collisions on the 1398 level crossings in the national rail network. Track operating authority OnTrack stressed that "trains have priority at level crossings and they cannot swerve or stop quickly to avoid accidents".

Yet, the average amount of level crossing accidents per year in the past ten years stands at 34, against on average 1800 injury road intersection collisions per year in the same period.

Asia

Asian nations, certainly those in the 'developing world', suffered many level crossing crashes between buses and trains, which perhaps points at a competition issue. With the increasing wealth of the tiger economies the problems at level crossings soared due to increasing car-ownership and with that came similar misbehaviour that was seen in the USA and Europe. The situation is technically dealt with in often exemplary modern ways (although the mix of older and modern equipment may look a bit confusing at times) whilst, contrary to the situation elsewhere in the world, judicial action resulting from incidents and accidents can be surprisingly hard on motorists who were caught out. A Taiwanese motorist caught after a level crossing offence, incident or accident my be fined between 6,000 and 12,000 Taiwanese dollars, a bicyclist 1,200 to 2,400 and a pedestrian 1,200 Taiwanese dollars. The solution to put new railway developments on viaducts to eliminate level crossings altogether can be seen in most of the modern urban areas of these countries as well, but the problems obviously remain with level crossings in the traditional lines in less intensely developed areas that, interestingly, like elsewhere in the world on average come down to a level crossing per one to two kilometres of track.

In Thailand a 10-ton tipper lorry went through the closed barriers into the side of a passenger train near Takli on the 20th of May 1988. The resulting derailment was aggravated by the coincidence that just past this level crossing there was a viaduct

Above: Vestiges of the old Japanese inspired black and yellow level crossing warning colours can be spotted at the post of the American outline crossbuck, but this thoroughly renewed installation, visited by a delegation of the Institution of Railway Signalling Engineers, has gone over to red and white. Please note the folding barrier boom, which stretches itself when the barriers close. The crossing keeper's hut is the white little pagoda at the opposite side of the crossing. *Archives W.J. Coenraad*

Above: The existing line crosses the road in the background with a manually operated level crossing, the new airport connection does so on a viaduct. A process of providing split level facilities to eliminate level crossings that can be seen throughout the world. In this case, however, the line on ground level will remain in use for freight and local rail traffic. *Archives W.J. Coenraad*

across an irrigation canal in which a number of the coaches fell. 27 people died.

Yet, with 38,000 level crossings (21,792 unmanned and 16,549 manned as per 31 March 2002) and a very complex sort of road traffic, India nevertheless ranked high among the safer nations with 0.10 level crossing accidents per million train kilometres in 2002. How this develops with its present high rate of motorisation remains to be seen, there are some entertaining videos on the Internet to illustrate the issue of the usual road user incompetence and misbehaviour, on level crossings, in that large nation.

Japan.

Japan suffered a few disastrous level crossing incidents with road freight vehicles:
• On the 9 November 1963 no less than 161 people were killed and 119 injured near Yokohama when a freight train derailed after being hit by a lorry at a multi-track level crossing and consequently fouled a number of other tracks without putting signals back to danger. As a result any train operator's worst nightmare came true; no less than two passenger trains with crush loads of Saturday night travellers ran into the wreckage at speed.
• In October 1970 the driver of a loaded tipper lorry ignored the warning of an AOC in the Isezaki line between Saginoniya and Hanasaki. An electric multiple unit train hit the vehicle, derailed and partially overturned. Five people were killed and 234 injured. This was the accident that sparked off a successful national action to improve level crossing safety.

What is surprising in Japan is to see how modern retro reflective and low-maintenance barrier booms appear to have as yet made little inroads. The nations barrier booms hardly ever fail to make a very minimal and often worn out impression. (Picture light loco's)

Europe

When comparing US and European figures it should be borne in mind that whilst the absolute mileage of roads and car-ownership ratio in the US are higher, traffic in Europe, both on the rails and the roads, is considerably denser due to the more compact and very heavily populated continent. Also, trains in Europe are on average more frequent and often faster than those in the USA. The average level crossing in Europe is therefore a rather busier place than one in the United States.

It rapidly became clear that the mass-motorisation, which started in Europe in the late 1950s and early 1960s (as against the 1920s in the USA), presented the rail operators not just with a profitability problem. The same variation in skills and attitudes in motorists that was noticed to blight safety on the level crossings in the USA from the 1920s onwards, appeared in Europe after World War 2 The increasing number of automatic level crossing of all types is where this problem quickly became manifest to the national traffic safety administrations.

Following the already mentioned accelerated introduction of automatic level crossings in the Netherlands since 1953, the situation deteriorated so quickly that in the sixties a film of an arranged crash on an AOC was screened on television to warn the population of what they risked. A similar exercise was staged in Britain at Hibaldstow level crossing in Lincolnshire early in 2007. Germany has declining level-crossing accident figures like its neighbouring nations, but observation by the author from the cab of a local train on a single-track line close to the Dutch border was not reassuring. It was noticed that at several different AHBs all types of road users kept moving

across (including a mother with a pram) until the train was very close indeed. The driver of the lightweight three-car articulated diesel-hydraulic multiple-unit train remarked laconically that it was very common and therefore it was not much use worrying about it. The situation was worse than had been observed in Britain, Switzerland or the Netherlands and its gravity was confirmed during other trips and subsequent talks on the subject in Germany.

Crossing misuse puts great stress on a train driver. As always with a train, apart from shutting off power, sounding the horn and initiating emergency braking, there is absolutely nothing else the driver can do but watch things go wrong. Level-crossing accidents and other vehicle intrusions onto the tracks are a serious danger, especially to the train driver fraternity.

Heavy freight

Comparatively there weren't as many disastrous crashes involving heavy road freight vehicles on level crossings in Europe as there were in the USA. Yet when they happened they were every bit as destructive.

On 9 December 1957 in Italy, a medium-sized Fiat 4.5-tonne road freight vehicle loaded with 3.5 tonnes of bagged clay approached a level crossing near Codogno station. It then stalled on the crossing, basically due to a lack of driver proficiency. As the driver restarted the engine, the remotely-operated barriers came down, but instead of driving through the barriers or using the available amount of space between the tracks (widening for the platforms at Codogno station) to try and get clear of the rails, the driver switched off the engine again and attempted with his co-driver to lift the barrier ahead of him. A woman on a bicycle offered her transport to get to the crossing keeper to have the barriers lifted, but the co-driver decided to run.

The 3 minutes and 3 seconds until the arrival of the train expired and the EMU, not booked to call at the station, hit the lorry at about 130km/h (80mph). For 150m the train remained on the track but then derailed on vehicle debris, swung out on the switch and crossing work for the station, crashed into a massive stone abutment of the station footbridge and rammed a mast of the electric catenary. The driver of the lorry, who stayed at the steering wheel of his vehicle awaiting the barriers to be opened for him, died. Also dead were 15 passengers on the train, whilst 11 passengers were badly injured.

Britain, a nation in doubt about the fundamental safety of automatic level crossings and late with their introduction, is where the first monster crash caused by road freight operators on an AHB level crossing in Europe took place. This was at Hixon, as recounted in Chapter 5.

Strangely enough, the Hixon accident had a late echo in an accident on 26 November 1993 at Kissimmee, Florida, USA. Amtrak's 'Silver Meteor' ran into a heavyweight gas-turbine electricity generator unit on a low-loader that had grounded on a level crossing. Again, failing preparations to secure safety, through sheer lack of foresight by those organising the trip, were identified as the main contributory causes.

France

France experienced a similar collision between a fast train and a road freight vehicle on an ADB level crossing, when on 8 July 1985 an 11-coach Corail push-pull train from Le Havre to Paris, doing 158km/h (almost 100mph) in push mode with the driving trailer leading, smashed into a low-loader at St Pierre-du-Vauvray. Of the 700 travellers on the train seven were left dead and 25 were badly injured, surprisingly low given the high-speed impact and derailment. It transpired that the low loader, going slow to check grounding risk, got caught out by the four lowering barriers. For some reason (see the Codogno accident in Italy above) the driver did not attempt to clear the crossing by driving through the closed barriers, unlike around 2,500 other motorists who do so in France every year.

As after the Polmont accident in Scotland on 30 July 1984, where a cow on the track derailed a push-pull operated Glasgow to Edinburgh service with the driving trailer leading, the wisdom and safety of high-speed push-pull operation and the safety of automatic level crossings without obstacle detection or interlock with signals was questioned.

Another disastrous crash occurred in France at St Foy-la-Gironde, west of Bordeaux on the line to Bergerac on 8 September 1997. Here, a loaded road tank vehicle accidentally went through the AHB and came to a stop on the track, to be hit by a two-car local train. The road freight vehicle exploded in a fireball, which developed into a fierce blaze and also involved nearby houses. The accident left 13 dead. The same circumstances as at Langenweddingen in East Germany 30 years earlier were at play; after hitting the tank vehicle, the whole train travelled through the erupting conflagration whilst braking, setting itself alight in the blazing fuel before coming to a stop further down the line.

On 22 June 2001, US road practice and European rail speed collided at Vilseck in Bavaria, Germany, when a US Army road freight vehicle did not stop at an AOC. This was on a single line through wooded countryside, and it was hit by a brand new two-car DMU with tilting body equipment, doing 140km/h or approx 85mph. Whilst a female soldier was able to jump off the truck before impact and survived, the train driver, lorry driver and a passenger died, whilst the remaining 24 of the 26 people on the train were injured.

The train did not derail and dragged the road vehicle wreck for about 200m (650ft) before coming to a stop and catching fire. A passenger reported the accident first with his mobile phone but the entire cab and front portion of the leading DMU vehicle burned out before the fire brigade arrived and were able to extinguish the flames.

Eleven hours later that same day four more people died and 15 people were injured during a second level crossing accident, this time at Tapfheim, also in Bavaria. Whilst the railways were not to blame for either, the German warning signal design was criticised due to questionable conspicuity. A few statistics came to light. In 1999, 412 level crossing accidents took 100 lives, but in 97% the blame rested with road users.

How do automatic level crossings work?

The basic operation sequence of an automatic level crossing, whether an automatic open crossing or an automatic half-barrier crossing, is dependent on the level-crossing equipment detecting a train that approaches, passes and then disappears into the distance. This detection is usually done with well-established equipment such as rail-treadles, axle counters, track circuits, wheel sensors and induction loops. All are used to run other automatic signalling equipment on the railway itself as well.

A treadle is a mechanical switch, fastened to the inside of the rail, which is actuated by the wheel flanges that keep the train on the track.

Axle counters used to work with the treadles mentioned above, but nowadays are devices that react to the magnetic fields of the train wheels passing by. The distinguishing feature of the axle counter is that the number of train wheels detected is stored in a

Above: Steinfurt-Borghorst AHB, Germany, with induction loops for train detection at the inside foot of the rail. *Peter van der Mark*

Above: Electro-mechanical rail treadle switch, France. *Peter van der Mark*

Above: Modern electro-magnetic rail switches of the type used for axle counters, Germany. *Peter van der Mark*

Above: An insulated rail joint separating two track circuits, Netherlands. *Peter van der Mark*

memory (counted in) after which the number is counted again at the end of the section (counted out). The number of wheels counted out has to tally with the number of wheels counted in. If the numbers do not match, the conclusion is that part of the train is still in section. Thus the signals will not revert to proceed and/or the crossing barriers will not lift.

A track circuit is an electrically-isolated section of track, through which a current is fed in an out-and-back electrical circuit using both rails. This keeps an electro-magnetic switch at the far end powered up and closed. This section is separated from similar neighbouring sections of track with insulated rail joints. If a train enters the section, the current is short-circuited from one rail to the other through wheels and axles, making the power to the switch drop and as a result it opens. This enables all sorts of automatic switching sequences to be set up, including operating an automatic level crossing. An additional advantage of the track circuit is that if the rail breaks, the circuit breaks and the power to the switch drops as well. Thus the associated signal does not revert to proceed when the last axle of the passing train leaves the track circuit concerned.

When the first axle of a train operates the detection device used for the automatic level crossing, it is said that the train 'strikes in'. After the train 'strikes in', a set sequence of actions on the level crossing starts, such as an initial warning of bells, warblers and flashing traffic signals. Then, after a set time, the barriers come down. After another minimum set time the train passes and 'strikes out'. The barriers start to lift. If another train has not struck in then after a set time the traffic signals will extinguish. With a run-of-the-mill type of European passenger train (two to six coaches at normal speeds of about 120 to 140km/h or 75 to 80mph) this whole sequence usually lasts less than one and a half minutes. The following, however, are important:

The train must run at a pre-determined maximum speed or less to avoid being at the crossing before it is properly closed.

It will be clear that slower trains will take longer to reach the crossing after 'strike-in' than the fastest trains.

What if the level crossing has failed?

As with all proper railway operations, the first issue to be considered with a level crossing that fails is that it will fail safe. It closes or shows the crossing as announcing a train coming, but will not show a false safe image to either the road user or the train driver. After that, rail operators have protocols in place to get traffic moving again in the safest possible way as soon as possible. A few examples follow.

In Britain no traffic moves, trains being stopped at the nearest signal, until a Network Rail official (the Movements Operations Manager or MOM) is in place with a key to operate the level crossing on instructions from the traffic controller. He will then inform the controller that the crossing is secured, after which the controller instructs the driver to pass the signal at Danger that covers the level crossing, and only then are trains allowed to move at severely reduced speed.

In Germany, the author experienced the Dutch driver of an ICE3 set on the way to Cologne receiving the order to move up to the failed level crossing near Emmerich, properly indicated with its kilometre identity, then stop, get off the train and close it with a key. After this, the train could pass. Unfortunately, the train failed to get door interlock on the door that the driver had used to alight and as a result of this on-board fault sat there for some time until the issue had been sorted out. Hassle for my colleague, slightly aggravated because of the many passengers watching our backs through the famous ICE3 window behind us, giving a forward view through the windscreen.

In the Netherlands, the joint authors were present in the cab of an electric locomotive hauling a 10-coach passenger train that had to negotiate three AHB level crossings between Eindhoven and 's-Hertogenbosch during an extensive signalling failure. The driver was informed of the situation ahead by radio and was instructed to pass certain failed signals at Danger and use a procedure that is known as '*aanrijden*' of the level crossings.

Every Dutch AHB has closure track circuits across the crossing. The 480-odd tonnes of train had to approach the crossing at very low speed to activate this track circuit and then stop. This initiated the closing sequence and following complete closure the train was allowed to proceed at reduced speed due to the signalling failure. One level crossing had two visibly nervous police constables who were keeping an eye on the rather fast-moving road traffic that showed no hesitation even when the front of the approaching locomotive was very close. That was indeed quite an experience for British-orientated railway people.

Safety of manual vs automatic level crossings

Manual barriers as such suffer from the inordinately expensive 'risk factor human being', who is responsible for many of the accidents on such crossings through falling asleep at odd times of the day and forgetting about or overlooking trains due to changed timetables, extra train services, pressure of work (especially on multi-track lines) and cutting corners with the procedures.

On the debit side of manual crossings one should notice that in case something goes wrong the crossing keepers are witnesses as well as the first source of information to the emergency services and they could intervene if the proper means to take drastic measures in a timely manner are put at their disposition, such as putting signals back to danger or using a direct radio connection with the cab of the approaching train. Furthermore, the rail operator puts the responsibility for safe operation fully within its own sphere of influence and has ways and means to instil and enforce (equipment logging recorders) minimum quality levels of operation from its employees. This is impossible where motoristsare concerned.

Manual barriers that are interlocked with signals are very safe indeed, but delay the road user significantly longer than the automatic crossings. Motorists will let the local crossing keeper know they are not amused. Abuse is rife and nations as diverse as Germany (a crossing keeper beaten unconscious by a freight vehicle driver and his mate in one case) and India (crossing keeper attacked by a mob) did not escape this scourge of violence based on literature and internet sources.

The following are typical examples of the crossing keeper risk problem.

At half past midnight on 3 August 1970 at Nunspeet, in the forested Veluwe region of the Netherlands, a self-propelled postal rail vehicle rammed a military minibus of which the fuel tank exploded, setting both the wreck and the train alight. Five military personnel were killed. It was proven that the manually-operated barriers were not closed and the driver of the minibus had actually stopped to let a freight past, but overlooked the postal service approaching from the opposite direction at about 120km/h (75mph). From the time of the night and from other indications it is assumed that the crossing keeper was asleep.

On 12 September 1982 a manually-operated level crossing near the Zürchersee (Lake Zurich), Switzerland, was the scene of a horrendous crash when the lady who operated the barriers of two very busy neighbouring level crossings appeared to have overlooked an approaching electrical multiple-unit train at 81km/h (50mph) and omitted to close the barriers. A German coach from Schönaich, on its way from Pfäffikon to Fehralthof at 55km/h (35mph approx), was hit broadside and was smashed into several parts. It caught fire, and that also set the crossing box alight. A passing motorist had the presence of mind to break in and drag the crossing keeper out. Thirty-nine passengers on the bus were left dead and the others badly injured. During the inquest the crossing keeper told of driver's aggressive behaviour if she kept the barriers closed a moment longer than the motorists thought necessary, but that day in all likelihood she fell asleep in the warm late summer weather. In the aftermath of this accident it transpired that throughout Europe the overlooking of trains by crossing keepers had been a cause for concern for a considerable time; the job is too monotonous and unchallenging.

SBB CFF FFS Swiss National Railways closed the last manually-operated level crossing in 1993; all the remaining secured public level crossings are automatic types.

The automatic level crossing is impermeable to boredom, forgetfulness, overlooking trains and other such traits of the under-challenged human brain. It has also proved extremely reliable in operation, fails safe and if treated with the necessary respect by everyone concerned is generally very safe indeed. With 'everyone concerned', though, lies the problem as indicated earlier.

The moment has now been reached where the rail network operators everywhere are attempting to take back the responsibility for safe operation. Typical examples are: eliminating manually-operated crossings with automatic crossings, substitution of AOCs with AHBs, and AHBs with ADBs. Some of these now have radar obstacle detection on the crossing surface. Many crossings themselves are eliminated by replacement with grade-separated crossings such as bridging or an underpass.

Only the latter, obviously, structurally eliminates the conflict of the level crossing, but it is also by far the most expensive solution and takes considerable time to put in place. Therefore it is unwise to ignore opportunities to provide level crossings as they are safer in the short term.

Who is at fault?

Official traffic safety figures issued in many European countries put 85-95% of the blame for level-crossing accidents squarely on the shoulders of the road users involved. The remaining 5-15% is accepted as blame on the rail network operator involved. These usually refer to mistakes at manually-operated crossings or mistakes made by rail operators when working under so-called degraded circumstances, such as during maintenance or during repairs of failed automatic crossings.

Of the blameworthy road users involved, 55-65% made an unconscious, genuine mistake or were involved in the consequences of the mistake of someone else. However, 35-45% made a conscious mistake in deciding to continue moving onto the level crossing whilst knowing that this would create massive danger to the safety of both themselves and others. Without fail, the worst offenders are younger people, with males outranking females approximately two or even three to one. A British Home Office report published in 2004 found that on average men commit nine times more traffic offences than women, and that what could be classed as sheer offensive behaviour causing an accident ranks highly among those transgressions. The offensive habit tails off markedly only in the 60-plus age groups. Retirement does seem to calm people down, or make them more sensible.

A typical accident where an inebriated youngish male car-driver thoroughly lost the plot happened on the evening of 25 December 1993 on an AHB in Zaandam in the Netherlands, when he suddenly overtook three waiting vehicles before him at the already closed half barriers. The car zigzagged onto the crossing and smashed at considerable speed into the nearside front bogie of the leading driving trailer of a 4-car double-deck push-pull train. The rail vehicle derailed and ended up against the concrete pier of a railway flyover, the three following coaches derailed, but the electric locomotive remained on the track. One train passenger was fatally injured and died, whilst a second one was badly injured. Eleven others were more or less slightly injured, among them being the train driver, the conductor and the car driver.

The majority of crossing accidents in Britain take place within a mile of the road user's home, which is a characteristic encountered in all nations that looked at this issue during the investigation of accidents. Offending road users were mostly well acquainted with the crossing; they either lived close to it or used it very regularly. Acknowledging the increased chance of meeting with an accident purely through regular presence at the crossing, nevertheless perhaps a case of familiarity breeding contempt?

An example of such a close to home accident on an AOC in the Netherlands, bringing other issues described earlier together, occurred on 3 November 2005 in the rural location of Wijhe when a road freight vehicle, ironically carrying materials to convert the AOC where the smash took place into an AHB, was driven onto the crossing against the warning and was hit by a double deck IRM EMU. This picked up the vehicle and dragged it along the track, derailing in the process and bringing the catenary down, but staying upright and in line. The 42-year-old truck driver had been on busy roads all day and was less than a few minutes from home; he lived within two kilometres of the crossing. He lost his life, four passengers on the train were badly injured and 33 slightly. The train driver vacated his cab before impact and survived.

Due to the above-mentioned high exposure reasons on the busiest crossings (road as well as rail traffic) these tend to chalk up the highest incident rates. But the main probable cause is that they tend to be closed more often as well as for longer periods due to multiple train passages. It is well known that this induces foolish behaviour. Clearly these are the first that should be replaced with grade-separated crossings.

Following are a few examples of serious accidents, where the railway itself clearly played a large role in what happened.

On 6 July 1967 a steam-hauled 8-car articulated double-deck hit a road tank vehicle on a very busy level crossing in

Below: The accident at Wijhe, Netherlands, in 2005. *Archive Prorail NL*

Above: Langenweddingen, Germany. The burnt-out double-deck coach sets with the remains of the road tanker beside them in the station platform, where the train came to a stop. The crossing is behind the photographer. *Archiv Erich Preuß*

Below: Italy is one of the very few nations where the Crossbuck or St Andrew's Cross is not a normal feature at all level crossings. Please note the new reflective barriers and instead of the crossbuck we can see a three-pointed star with red lenses at its tips, which in earlier days would revolve when the barriers descended. It looks very much like a four-pointed (crossbuck-like) star of similar construction, which at one time was a regular feature on crossings manufactured by a particular factory in the USA. Which is where this crossing equipment clearly has its roots. *Peter van der Mark*

Langenweddingen, near Magdeburg in East Germany, causing the eruption of a blaze that engulfed the still-moving train and the signalbox. It was caused by a bizarre failure of the manual double barriers, the tip of one barrier getting caught behind a nearby sagging telephone cable, which prevented its lowering. The possibility of this happening had been noticed ever since the former full-barrier layout had been replaced with double barriers after a bus had rammed the equipment, but this wasn't acted upon. Furthermore, on the day of the accident, had a previously arrived steam-hauled freight from the opposite direction been dealt with as prescribed by lowering the barriers in case the train overshot, as the crossing was within the stop signal overlap, the snag would possibly have shown up earlier and the accident might not have happened at all.

However, on noticing the barriers would not come down, instead of throwing the already cleared signals (not in all cases is there interlock between signals and level-crossing barriers in Germany) back to Danger or getting out to warn motorists to stay away, the panicking signaller kept attempting to lower the barriers. Whilst most of the motorists, including a freight vehicle, stopped because of the less than half lowered barriers and the frantic waving with a flag by the signaller in the last moments before impact, the tank vehicle driver only slowed down and then accelerated onto the crossing right in the path of the approaching passenger train. That still almost missed the vehicle, as it was only the right hand buffer of the locomotive that tore open the tank, after which the conflagration erupted. The accident killed no fewer than 94, 50 adults (one of whom a man who brought 12 children out of a burning carriage but succumbed to his own

Below: St Aignan, France. Barely have the barriers of this ADB level crossing started to rise than the first car is on the crossing. *Peter van der Mark*

Above: Big-city suburbia in Japan. An EMU has just arrived and the ticket examiner is ready to collect the tickets whilst the barriers of the AHB have just opened and people are crossing the tracks. If anyone from the left ventures to cross with closed barriers in this situation, assuming it is the just arrived train we see that keeps the barriers closed, then there is no chance to spot a train coming through the station until it is too late, especially if that train comes through at speed. *Milepost 92½*

burns injuries the next day) and 44 children of a group on their way to a holiday camp. The accident caused signals to be resited and to be interlocked with the barriers.

On 26 September 1999 at McLean, Illinois, a northbound Amtrak service from St Louis, Missouri, to Chicago, Illinois, hit a car on a level crossing on US route 136. The car driver and his passenger were killed, whilst the train remained unscathed and no one was hurt. It transpired that neither of the flashing warning lights for the crossing had worked, nor had the barriers lowered. A fitter had worked on the warning installation of the crossing and failed to remove an earth jumper wire from the crossing control relay and omitted to ensure the proper working of the installation after finishing his work, as prescribed in writing by the Union Pacific Railroad.

On 26 June 2000 at Hudson, Louisiana, several road users, among them the driver of a tank vehicle, had to make emergency manœuvres to avoid colliding with a local freight on a level crossing. An articulated road freight vehicle loaded with logs ran into the lead locomotive and logs entering his cab fatally injured the train driver. The front bogie of the locomotive derailed, but it stayed upright and travelled another 101ft (approximately 30m) along the track before coming to a stop. According to witnesses the warning lights of only one side of the approaches to the level crossing had activated, the others remained off. The day before the accident electrical storms had raged in the area and power cuts had been experienced, which according to witnesses had caused the warning lights of the crossing to activate spuriously and then turn off again.

This was substantiated by video images from the security system of a pipeline control station, which showed that they had worked continuously through the night. It was also found that although many motorists stopped at the crossing before moving on, many just continued without slowing down. The same was

later reported from other, similar crossings in the area. A snarl-up in communication between the police and the railway signalling maintainers caused no fitters to be sent out to check the crossings. As the level-crossing equipment was destroyed in the accident it was impossible to determine its state of health and functionality.

On 31 October 2002 two electricians performed unscheduled repairs to an AHB near Veenendaal in the Netherlands, which is situated on quite a sharp curve. The road itself makes a sharp turn to reach the level crossing. Without proper consultation with the controlling signallers, they switched off the AHB installation and as a result the equipment did not secure the crossing when EC-3 *Rembrandt* approached at speed. An unfortunate coincidence was that a private car as well as a road freight vehicle were on the crossing when the 80-tonne electric locomotive struck, whereby the private car was flattened between the locomotive and the lorry, killing the driver. The two electricians were apprehended and convicted for gross negligence.

Issues to consider

The following attempts to explain the most common causes at the root of level-crossing accidents.

First, road users tend to approach the railway level crossing in the same fashion as they do a road intersection. This is based on the perceived risk versus their estimated capability to deal with it,

Right: An AHB crossing on the
splendid rapid-transit network in
Calgary, Alberta, Canada. The
inadvertently slightly leaning barrier
on the left side is visually much more
easily picked up than the fully
vertical barrier on the right. This
crossing suffers from a lack of
conspicuity to the road user.
Peter van der Mark

percieved risk, which is no different from the process leading for instance to the frequent jumping of the traffic lights at road intersections. Perceived risk is quite different from actual, objective risk. The perception of risk and the split-second decisions following from it are influenced by mental characteristics of the person involved, by what is visible and audible on location and by what is known about risks in this particular set of circumstances, *e.g.* through previously gained experience or through other sources of knowledge.

In past years a number of articles have appeared in the media concern being average eyesight and hearing of a substantial number of people behind the steering wheel of road vehiclesbeing defective. As a consequence the perception of risk in many is based on information from sensory faculties with questionable properties. This would probably explain why for instance a low sun in the eyes appears rather often as a last-ditch explanation for a level-crossing accident and that warning bells or warblers (bleepers) weren't heard.

Even if that actually was the case and the warning signs and the approaching train could not be properly seen for that reason, the obvious question remains as to why the road user entered the level crossing at all under those circumstances instead of stopping and making sure.

Entering the level crossing with warning signals working as well as not waiting until the barriers are fully open and the signal lights are extinguished is the single biggest reason for fatal accidents on AOCs and AHBs. This results from a lack of time to correct the initial mistake by getting out of the way of the fast approaching train. The biggest injury/fatality groups in these cases are cyclists and pedestrians. They usually commit a conscious mistake by entering the crossing too quickly after the passage of a first train, without waiting for a (perhaps none too clearly announced) second approaching train. In particular, stations close to a level crossing tend to cause this type of accident, as the road user thinks that the train in the platform is the one that keeps the crossing closed, disregarding the possibility of an approaching train along another track. Furthermore, a train in a platform generates risk-taking in people who want to catch it and often it hinders the view of a second train approaching the crossing from the opposite direction.

Most nations recognise a link between the waiting times from the start of lowering of the barriers until the moment the train is at the crossing versus road users starting to cross against the warning. The shorter this waiting time, the less likely it is that drivers will take risks. It is, on the other hand, often hard to distinguish manual level crossings, where one will have to wait a longer time, from the automatic half-barrier version where the whole sequence from closure to reopening of the barriers or extinguishing of the warning lights may take less than two minutes. This might be one reason that induces motorists to keep going when the automatic crossing barriers are closing.

Many crossings with high approach speeds by road traffic, especially through a curve or with less than a 90° angle between the road and the tracks, are dangerous. As much as motorists are generally unaware of train speeds, they are often equally unaware of how fast their own vehicle actually travels and what their necessary braking distance will be under all circumstances. Additionally, many motorists do not take many other issues to account than the road immediately ahead of them when deciding about the speed of their car; the further they can see their road is clear the faster they will go. This stresses the importance of the conspicuity of the warning given by the level-crossing road signals.

In France, interestingly, this phenomenon of motorists not noticing dangerous road features further ahead brought about a short curve in the road just before coming onto a roundabout, forcing motorists to bring the speed down. France was also the nation that successfully introduced the inward-leaning crossing barriers in the open position, to make the level crossing more conspicuous in its surroundings.

However, on such crossings with high road speed approaches it isn't only the first motorist at the barriers who causes the danger. Many a waiting motorist was hit from behind by a following vehicle and pushed on to the crossing in the path of a train, as it happens on road intersections. This danger is aggravated by the bad habit of many keeping the car in gear and holding it with the brake pedal. When hit, even relatively slowly, the car will then actually drive itself well onto the crossing before the surprised and shaken motorist has again regained control.

Many people tend to drive close to the preceding vehicle in circumstances of dense traffic, and will not be aware of traffic jams

further ahead until the brake lights of the immediately preceding vehicle light up. If that happens on a level crossing there is acute danger; quite a few have paid with their lives for this folly. Worse, some of these motorists were bus or lorry drivers and they were responsible for many deaths and injuries on their own vehicles and on the colliding train.

If in this situation the barriers start to come down, though, most of the more alert private car drivers manage to get out of their vehicles and vacate the level crossing.

People get caught on crossings with full- or double-barrier protection. It is for them that automatic crossings were designed, with half barriers to allow escape. The habit of many, however, is to use this feature to zigzag past the barriers. This led to a reconsideration of the full-barrier protection to close off the entire crossing. As the accidents at Codogno and St Pierre-du-Vauvray proved, in some cases the trapped motorist does not think of driving through the closed barriers (which are all designed to snap off in such circumstances). Therefore, on the modern variety of automatic

Left: To show an old US AHB installation we visit Chile, on a railway line that has been taken out of use. It has all the elements that make up such an installation; the 'crossbuck' sign (still used throughout the English-speaking world for cross or crossing) made up of two planks, the half barrier and the two alternating red flashing lights that replaced the electro-mechanical wigwag signal, all mounted to a single post. Simple design, tried and tested, copied the world over. *Archiv IRSE*

Below: The station at Calpe, Spain, along the narrow-gauge coastal railway line from Alicante northward to Denia. We see the signal that tells the driver that the road signals of the AOC ahead are working correctly and that he is permitted to pass the crossing. The S-board before the crossing is a whistle board. *Peter van der Mark*

Right: An AOC in Sweden sports the same parts that we saw before on a Dutch AOC (page 99) and yet it doesn't look at all like it. National ideas and customs play a large part in how equipment like a level crossing presents itself to the users.
Peter van der Mark

Below: The language problem. This telephone with sign on a French ADB gives very useful information about what to do in case of failure (it even mentions what should be considered a failure), what to say to the controller and how to detour past the failed crossing. One has to read and speak French to be able to deal with it, though. Standardising this sort of equipment throughout Europe should have priority.
Peter van der Mark

double-barrier level crossings, some form of obstacle detection has to be provided that normally will open the exit barriers if obstacles on the crossing surface within a clearly defined grid are detected. Radar is very successfully used for this purpose. For pedestrians and cyclists, escape bays of some sort are usually provided.

Not many are aware that the vast majority of rail vehicles (including light rail) have been legally vested with priority in situations of conflicting right of way with road traffic where no traffic signals have been provided. In mainland Europe motorists involved in level-crossing accidents have been known to invoke the infamous 'priority from right' rule as their reason to continue; the train, coming from the left, ought to have stopped. People on the whole have little notion of train speeds and the long braking distances that fast or heavy trains need to come to a stop. Also, strange as it may seem, many people are unaware that trains are unable to swerve or make other avoiding manoeuvres.

Level crossing design

Most automatic level crossings in Europe and Asia owe much of their looks to US practice. This applies especially to the traditional ones in Belgium, the Netherlands and those in Japan, Russia and the former Soviet Union, Italy, and many African and Far Eastern nations. Others show the traditional European single flashing light feature one finds for example in France and Germany.

The alternating flashing warning lights go back to the US wigwag automatic grade-crossing warning signal. This is essentially made up of a post with a bracket from which originally a short horizontal bar was suspended that at its lower end had a disc. When a warning to the road users about an approaching train was initiated, an electro-mechanical device made this bar and disc move from side to side in a rocking motion, which in good sighting circumstances was quite an eye-catching way of getting the warning message across. It was superseded by the two alternately flashing red lights.

Not only the road user but also the train driver may have

crossing signals, in this case called crossing monitoring signals. Often they show a white (flashing) light to indicate a safe passage and a yellow or red light to indicate problems ahead. If the white coloured light doesn't show, the train has to be slowed down with the emergency brake, hopefully coming to a stop before reaching the crossing. Furthermore, the crossing may be interlocked with the actual section signals for the train. If the crossing can't be properly closed, the signal will keep showing a red aspect.

The presentation and types of level crossings throughout Europe to the road user depend on national custom and design and for that reason are sometimes inconsistent from nation to nation. For instance, the shape and nature of the indications, flashing rates and intensity of the warning lights differ in a number of countries. Also, types of level crossings differ. This might make noticing the presence of a level crossing or dealing with some of the national variations by foreigners a problem.

Some nations also have differing sequences of warning signs leading up to a level crossing as well as light signal sequences accompanying the warning for crossing closure and an approaching train, although the types of signs and signals used are usually the same as used for other traffic situations. Some use the normal traffic lights; others use a single red flashing light. There are networks that show a yellow flashing light before showing the red flashing lights.

This issue is made less important, as described earlier, by the fact that in Europe it has been noticed that the majority of people involved in accidents on level crossings actually live near or use that level crossing regularly, e.g. on the way to and from work. They knew where the level crossing was.

Then there is the problem that some foreign car-drivers come from virtually rail-free nations and have very little understanding of what crossing a railway line actually means with respect to their personal safety.

A bigger problem might be that there is the need to speak the local language well, in order to contact rail traffic controllers by telephone, or to read and interpret the signs in order to secure safe passage on some types of level crossings. This adds considerably to the problem of the variety in presentation.

Like traffic signs and a number of internationally used railway signs, the level crossing types and the way they present the approach of a train to the road user should be better standardised.

Derailment and how to mitigate the chance of it happening

Whilst in North America, Western Europe and Japan the number of level-crossing accidents and casualties is tackled with considerable success, the fact is that deliberate actions of some motorists (including suicides) will continue to pose a threat to train safety, not mentioning other vehicles intruding into the rail kinetic envelope accidentally (falling from roads and bridges or rolling onto the track) or through vandalism.

Trains have to be made more resistant to derailment following impact; they must be capable of meeting a known safety problem with the least amount of danger to passengers or freight. From an operational point of view it is advantageous to keep the train as damage-free and intact as possible, able to be moved away on its own wheels or even under its own power, to keep costly downtime of train and track to a minimum.

The body of a motor vehicle at the front end of a still moving train often crumples up into a fairly solid object that then disappears under the train's frame to interfere with the motion of the front bogie frame and the wheels. The wreck, when obstructed

Above: On 13 July 1998 a two-car EMU working a local service from Eindhoven to Weert, Netherlands, hit a farm tractor virtually at the end of its trip. The first bogie derailed toward the other track just as a freight train passed by and ripped out the side of half a coach. It is an illustration of the danger of derailment caused by a level-crossing accident. The item on the track in front of the train, incidentally, is the cab of the tractor. The tunnel that replaced this AOC was virtually finished at the time of this accident. *Archive Prorail NL*

by track features, may lift a modern lightweight rail vehicle off the track. Furthermore, road vehicle driveline fittings such as axles and wheels, drive train, transmission and engine block disintegrate, shedding rather solid pieces of metal between the train wheels and the railhead.

Either way, a locomotive, leading coach or indeed the whole train, may very well be derailed before the train comes to a stand. As the rails not only carry but also 'steer' the train, the feature that defines railways, derailment takes all control of the train away from the driver and causes havoc if the derailing train overturns, hits turnouts, lineside structures or enters the kinetic envelope of another track into the path of another train, never mind falling off a bridge or embankment.

A recent feature on European trains to deal with this danger is the obstacle deflector. Earlier it was known as the cowcatcher, the cattle guard or the pilot beam and the person credited with the first application is Isaac Dripps, master mechanic of the Camden & Amboy Railroad Co, New Jersey, USA. He fitted the steam locomotive *John Bull* (imported from Britain and now in the Smithsonian collection in Washington DC) with this contrivance in 1833. Whilst this was because of cattle roaming the countryside freely, later in the 1920s a similar fitting to the front end of trains proved successful in keeping cars from endangering the train.

In Continental Europe the usefulness of a truly capable obstacle deflector was rediscovered in the Netherlands following a costly derailment of an electric multiple-unit train after a level-crossing accident in the marshy countryside near Driebruggen on 30 March 1988. A complete derailment and overturning of a 4-car diesel-hydraulic multiple-unit train that ran into a herd of cows on the track near Tietjerk in the province of Friesland a few years later clinched it and at present virtually all Dutch passenger rolling stock has been fitted with obstacle deflectors under the nose ends, whilst new builds of rolling stock must have an obstacle deflector incorporated by European law. In the USA the author has noticed remote control cars (driving trailers) in double-deck push-pull commuter trains around Chicago, Illinois, that were fitted with the unmistakable massive Dutch obstacle deflector.

This type of obstacle deflector is designed to withstand the impact of a passenger car, a sizeable rock or tree trunk or that of large cattle like a cow or bull (set at 1,000kN) without deformation at speeds of 100km/h or 60mph. It is not allowed to break or shear off and further endanger the train through ending up under its wheels or inhibit the motion of the front bogie. It must keep the obstacle in front and not push it aside where another train may hit it.

In Norway, on recent series of electric multiple-unit rolling stock the entire nose of the train is designed as an obstacle deflector, to do all the things described above. Additionally, it is shaped to avoid throwing large wild animals up into the electric catenary wires, to avoid pantograph dewirements and so cause crippling and costly damage to train and energy transmission hardware in remote places where assistance is not quickly at hand. One may dispute the aesthetic merits, but the effectiveness is proven.

In Britain, obstacle deflectors may be spotted on the Class 180, the successful Class 222 and 223 diesel-electric multiple-unit sets (which have all been fitted with a hinged deflector for rail-head clearance reasons when travelling with the secondary suspension air bellows deflated) and on the Class 373 'Eurostars'.

The result is that with trains so fitted, derailments after impact with private cars and light road freight vehicles have virtually disappeared. Only when a car runs into the broadside of a train (not unknown!) may the derailment of an intermediate coach take place.

Obviously, road freight vehicles are still a menace through their mass and the nature of their cargoes. Also, through the height of their chassis frames the obstacle deflector is often not effective as they engage with the front end of the train above frame height. This can be seen in the picture of the Wijhe accident in the Netherlands earlier in this book.

Excessive braking in an emergency

A further danger to trains involved in level-crossing incidents is derived from the braking effort when the driver of a long train composed of a mixture of vehicles selects the emergency braking position of his brake valve. It deals with the way in which a train, using the normal air brake, actually brakes.

Braking a train with the normal air brake starts from the front end, where air in the train brake pipe is vented through the driver's brake valve. Gradually the brakes apply from the front to the rear, a process called the propagation of the brake. On long trains this may take its time and the front of the train can be braking hard already when the rear is still rolling freely and therefore starts bunching up against the front end. For this reason, it is North American practice to keep the locomotive pulling until the brake works throughout the whole train.

In reverse, when closing the brake valve to bring the brake pipe back to release pressure, the release of the brakes starts again from the front. This means that the brakes at the front of the train may be released already when the brakes at the rear of the train are still applied. Hurried drivers putting full power on to their locomotives in this situation (red signals coming off to yellow or green are well known to induce this situation) may rip out couplers and break the train. This was not rare in the days of long mixed freights in Europe.

The following happened for the above-mentioned reason, sourced from the website of the Transportation Safety Board of Canada:

On October 6, 2001 a Canadian National mixed freight train was on the way to Moncton, New Brunswick, with three locomotives at the front, 60 loaded cars, 52 empty cars and 18 so-called residue tank cars. The train weighed in at approximately 10,000 tons and the data recorder logged a speed of 38mph, approx 60km/h, with the power controller in notch 8, which is full power on a rising gradient. On approaching a farm crossing, the train driver saw a car approaching the crossing close in front of him, move onto it and then stop. The train driver sounded the horn and when it became clear that the car had stalled on the crossing he applied the emergency brake and took shelter with his conductor. The lead locomotive struck the car, vacated in time by the occupants, and then stopped 1,070ft (a good 300m), past the crossing.

Importantly, one piece of emergency braking equipment had not been operated. It is incorporated in the Train Information and Braking System (TIBS) with which many North American trains are equipped and which includes an emergency brake toggle switch on the traction control console, which remotely controls a brake pipe valve at the rear of the train and applies the brakes from the rear as well.

When police cars approached the accident area police officers smelled gas and withdrew immediately, adhering to their safety training. When people in protective gear finally moved in, they found that the 63rd and the 88th to the 101st car had been derailed. The 63rd vehicle, an empty tank car, was literally folded upwards into an A shape. The cars further to the rear had rolled over, while two long automobile carriers had jack-knifed and six loaded tank cars with LPG had piled up behind them. From the 95th tank car butane was venting, which the officers had smelled and which rightly had induced them to vacate the site.

During investigation it was found that the front of the train, behind the locomotives, was where many empty vehicles were travelling, whilst most of the loaded vehicles in the train had been marshalled towards the rear. The mix of long and short cars was a matter of 'where whatever ended up was wherever it remained'. The heavy brake application and its propagation effect mentioned earlier, exacerbated by hill climbing which stretched all the coupler springs, made the heavy tail end of the train roll unchecked into the already braking lighter front end and so exert enormous pressure. This caused the derailment and other damage.

Learning the lessons

Studying the accident histories and the reports about improving safety on level crossings, a number of parallel conclusions emerge with international validity. These are the most important ones.

1 Better and more focused education; the role of the media

There is little doubt that the stream of articles in the media following a number of high profile level-crossing accidents in the early 21st century in Europe, Australia and the USA had a beneficial effect on level-crossing safety through focusing public attention on the potential for damage and death that exists. The record low score for level-crossing accidents in 2006 in the Netherlands and Great Britain as well as the experience in Australia, where idiosyncratic behaviour of road freight drivers leading to some very damaging crashes attracted ridicule in the media, also backs up this impression. The positive attention the media gave to the subject had an educating effect.

It showed potential perpetrators of level crossing mischief that acceptance was running out and it brought to the attention of the population in general how a level-crossing accident brought misery and grief to many through the misconduct of one person. Quite important was additionally that the blame rested wholly on the road user; there was no way in which 'the railway' could be blamed. The media attention increased the knowledge of road users and influenced the perceived risk factors.

The same counts, obviously, for school education. It is important to be taught about the dangers of the railway, level crossings and the dangers of being ignorant on and around them. It is sad, therefore, that too many children still learn the facts of life on the railway through getting caught out, often being extremely stupid when 'playing chicken' with trains. They effortlessly escape the train with which they play chicken, but usually miss the other train bearing down on them behind their backs along the track they step on. After such an event right in front of their friends the crossing is usually safe for a couple of years.

I would like to explain to children the futility of daring a train in the following way. A train may weigh anything from 40 to 4,000 tonnes or more and may do any speed up to 168mph. Even at much lower speeds than that, a train simply cannot be stopped in time; it cannot swerve around them, it will go straight for them. They either get smashed like a bug by a swat if they're lucky (because then there is usually still something for their parents to look at) or get mashed like beef in the meat grinder and then they'll fit in a plastic bucket or a plastic waste bin liner.

This rough but easily visualised comparison usually gets the message through to them, as most do not realise what their family would have to go through if things went wrong and the worst came true. When being told straight, most take note.

2 Automatic double barriers with obstacle detection

Taking back maximum responsibility for level-crossing safety is one way in which the rail operators attempt to diminish the number of accidents. In the Netherlands it was calculated that AHBs are safer than AOCs by a factor of 10, which means that instead of an accident every three years there will be an accident every 30 years. It led to converting all AOCs to AHBs, as many other European nations are now doing.

The ultimate safe crossing is the grade-separated bridge or tunnel, but the ultimate safe level-crossing is the manual or automatic double barrier level crossing. This crossing has four barriers across both traffic lanes at both sides of the railway tracks, whereby the exit barriers close a fraction later than the entry barriers, so momentarily permitting escape. This layout tackles the consciously committed mistakes by making zigzagging onto the level crossing impossible without causing conspicuous damage to vehicle and crossing. The responsibility for the safety on the crossing is virtually completely back in the hands of the rail operator.

The only issue, with quite a few examples in history showing its tenacious existence, is the danger of locking in road users on the crossing between the barriers. That is being

Below: The AOCs in the Netherlands have all been replaced with AHBs. This photograph illustrates such a conversion. The barriers are of the new aluminium type with in-built flashing LED lights whilst the actual traffic signals also have LED light sources, flashing at a high rate. There is nothing inconspicuous about this AHB crossing. *Peter van der Mark*

Right: In Germany too the conspicuity of level-crossing equipment has been drastically improved following criticism. Here, at Steinfurt-Borghorst, we see the result, complete with the leaning open barriers that follow French practice. Note also the separate crossings for cyclists and pedestrians. *Peter van der Mark*

Right: In Germany too the conspicuity of level-crossing equipment has been drastically improved following criticism. Here, at Steinfurt-Borghorst, we see the result, complete with the leaning open barriers that follow French practice. Note also the separate crossings for cyclists and pedestrians. *Peter van der Mark*

addressed with automatic detection of obstacles on the crossing, which lifts the exit barriers if something is noticed in the detection field. Other features are escape bays for pedestrians and cyclists to get away from the crossing surface.

3 Better warning lights, LEDs with high flash rates, more conspicuous reflective barriers with flashing lights

From the text, it should be clear that it is the warning of an approaching train that is the most important indication that the level-crossing equipment should transmit to the road user. It is important to ensure that the equipment used does so clearly, unmistakably and reliably in the midst of visual clutter, with warning signals that outperform the

surrounding 'white noise'. One solution is to equip the crossing with so-called LED (Light Emitting Diode) signals, set at a higher flashing rate than possible with the traditional tungsten light bulbs.

There are several advantages to LEDs, small devices that come in cluster assemblies called matrixes. Except in case of a complete power failure or complete destruction, they never fail all at the same moment. Therefore the operating reliability of LED signals is very high. Their light output can be fine-tuned to the ambient circumstances, while it is possible to fit various colour light LEDs into one signal head matrix so that all signal light colours may show through one lens. The glass or Plexiglas lens covering the LED assembly is not coloured,

Right: Wolfheze AHB, Netherlands. The photograph shows the kerbing put in to hinder zigzagging. Note the obsolete type of wooden barriers, now being replaced at a high rate with the new aluminium retro-reflective ones that lean inward when open as per French practice. *Peter van der Mark*

so during strong, low angle lighting by the winter sun the phantom aspect will not be coloured and so mislead the motorist or train driver. Last but not least, LEDs switch on and off instantaneously, where tungsten light bulbs 'glow' on and off, which enables quick and vision-arresting flashing rates to be used. Other light sources that could be considered for this role are the multi-flash strobe lights or revolving mirror lights that are used on police cars, for example.

The same applies to barriers used. They used to be manufactured from painted steel tube or wood that required regular repainting to keep the colours fresh, but the modern versions are made of lightweight plastic or aluminium and are covered in very durable reflective plastic foils in highly conspicuous colours that glow in the glare of car headlights during darkness and fog. On top of that, LED clusters may be fitted in the barriers that flash in unison with the main warning lights.

4 Separating the traffic lanes with kerbs to obstruct zigzag manœuvres, and paving features such as noise asphalt and narrowing roadways, speed humps and a raised traffic table at the crossing surface

Whilst most of the accidents with motor vehicles happen due to various oversights and mistakes, there is a category that is due to people taking deliberate risk when zigzagging around the closed half barriers. There is no way in which this behaviour can be eliminated unless it is physically made impossible or very hard to execute.

The idea was born to separate the traffic lanes of the road leading up to the level crossing with kerbing. This forces most motorists who are thinking about zigzaging around the barriers to slow down while negotiating the kerbing, which makes the venture that much riskier through time loss, they normally will not do it.

In order not to lock cars in a line in case of a stalled vehicle ahead, however, the kerbing has to be negotiable by vehicles. In Britain something quite similar was advertised recently but plastic poles on the kerbing were added to make the visual deterrent to do silly things even greater. Again, driving over them flattens the poles. Obviously, kerbing is also used to make the traffic lanes visually narrower to even more increase the perceived risk, which slows traffic down. For the same reason speed humps are put in just before the crossing and the crossing surface itself can be made into a raised traffic table. Noise asphalt, moulded in little bumps or ridges, is also used to set up an audible warning and make the steering wheel judder lightly, which further increases the perceived risk. In Australia it warns drivers of nearby open crossings in circumstances of bad vision ahead.

5 Physical barriers to stop road vehicles
One of the more interesting issues of the present time is news about ways of dealing with problems that we all are acquainted with, coming from places like the former Soviet republics and Eastern European nations. A solution from the former Soviet Union to prevent road vehicles entering the level crossing is a set of barriers coming up from the road surface under the normal 'boom' barriers, quite akin to similarly functioning but smaller road surface 'flap' barriers we know in Europe to prevent motorists from entering certain areas in one direction but allow others out in the opposite direction.

Their value certainly lies in the deterrent effect. When smashing into them one won't drive away unnoticed, even if the vehicle is still movable at all. But it looks doubtful whether these barriers will bring the vehicles with the highest risk to trains, heavy road freight vehicles at speed, to a full stop before they and their cargo foul the crossing area. What is quite thought provoking, though, is what must have happened on a level crossing that made these safety measures appear an acceptable solution. According to sources they are quite widespread in some locations.

In the USA it is said that there are heavy barrier structures rising out of the road or rolling in from the roadside, though little more is known to the author. It seems unlikely that these devices will ever satisfy safety authorities in Europe.

6 Enforcing co-operation, traffic cameras and prosecution
One of the complaints from the rail operators is the lack of co-operation by the judiciary in many countries when prosecuting a level-crossing offender. Australian newspapers and organisations raised complaints about it and similar noises can be heard in Britain, where people who caused great danger to others through reckless behaviour in their road vehicles were let off with barely an audible slap on the wrist. When caught and convicted after causing danger to others for no particularly valid reason, only a correctional measure that seriously hurts will cause the offenders to take note and reconsider their future behaviour.

The educational angle: if perhaps the traffic camera didn't deter someone one day but the road user was apprehended on the evidence presented, the pictures taken of what happened at that crossing might show the offending road user the stupidity of his behaviour, when he had to hurriedly back off or shot across just in time. Otherwise, images and sounds of a real accident might be harrowing enough to induce second thoughts on the subject of a future crossing against the warning. Therefore, previously recorded incident and accident pictures that are available should be used for educational purposes, to show apprehended offenders what could have happened and what they exposed others in their

Below: Platform barrow and foot crossings, especially when used by passengers to go from one platform to the other, are a grave source of danger. The two boxes are in fact warning lights to announce an approaching train, but strangely enough they are coloured green. On the other side, the text on the warning lights (STOP) is understandable by most speakers of European languages. *Peter van der Mark*

Right: This signal at Arnhem, Netherlands, is controlled by vehicle detection loops at the opposite side of the level crossing. If these loops detect jamming traffic then the yellow LED lights in the corners start to flash as similar signs do along motorways and the message 'Keep Crossing Clear' lights up in white. Although the ubiquitous graffiti taggers had to have a go, apparently they respected the important function of this sign. *Peter van der Mark*

car to. If the fate of the people in that recorded accident keeps others from doing what they did, at least they did not entirely die in vain.

7 'Second train approaching' warning

One of the big problems at automatic level crossings is to keep people from entering after a train has just passed the level crossing but before the signals stop working or the barriers are fully lifted. The danger may be that of a second train on another track, mostly but not necessarily from the opposite direction to the first one. If the road-traffic signals do not indicate that, then there is a fair chance that people are going to get hurt, as has happened many times in many nations.

Many ideas have been put forward to indicate a second train coming. These include synthesised voice calling out (but one has to speak the local language then) or different sounding bells. In the Netherlands, when the first train 'strikes in' the bells will ring very loudly for a moment and then go to about half volume when the barriers are down, which is maintained for the duration of the closure. If, however, a second train 'strikes in' the bells will revert to their full volume for an extended moment and then reduce in volume again.

8 Split the crossing into several pathways for different kinds of traffic

Many level crossings are not only the place where the railway tracks and the road intersect; they are also the often narrow place where a lot of different types of road traffic in two directions pass close to each other, slow traffic hindering faster traffic. There is the primary danger of the trains as well as the secondary danger that motor vehicles may hit pedestrians and cyclists through moving over the middle line and squeeze traffic in the opposite direction; motor vehicles

may run off the crossing deck onto the track and get stuck. The chance that a road traffic accident occurs on a level crossing is not at all rare.

In many Northern and North West European regions cyclists and pedestrians have been separated from motorised traffic by means of footpaths and bicycle lanes. For reasons of level-crossing safety, this separation is often extended across the level crossing, whereby the bicycle and pedestrian lanes have their own barriers that are worked from the rear of the main barrier pedestals. This clears the vehicle traffic flow of hindrance by slower traffic and protects the cyclists and pedestrians from the danger of getting under the wheels of big vehicles.

Above: A tourist steam train of an organisation preserving industrial narrow gauge rolling stock passes a level crossing with one of Holland's bicycle paths at a very leisurely pace. The location is the coastal dunes at Valkenburg near The Hague. Still a place where everybody concerned should keep a good lookout and a set of crossbucks would perhaps add to safety as well as enhance the rail atmosphere. *Peter van der Mark*

9 Warning to stay off the crossing in case of threatened traffic jam ahead

It was mentioned earlier that in traffic jams a row of cars might come to a halt across a level crossing, despite signs that the crossing should be kept clear. An electronic device has been developed to try and avoid this situation. It consists of the type of boards as used on motorways to announce traffic jams ahead, with alternating flashing yellow lights in the corners and a flashing optical fibre illuminated warning for the traffic jam and to keep the level crossing clear. The system measures road occupancy at the exit side of the level crossing with detection loops and if this occupancy leaves less free road space than a set length of space it will start warning traffic at the approach side of the level crossing. The results so far are positive.

10 Electronic warning devices working on radio or radar scanners in cars

Australia and the USA have developed systems that use the radar scanner that many motorists have to warn for speed checks, to indicate the approach to a level crossing when warning for an approaching train. The background is to mitigate against a number of crashes where especially road freight vehicles actually drove at speed into the side of a train at open crossings, notably during darkness or fog or a combination of the two. In Europe level crossings where this could be a problem are usually well indicated by active protection features and in Britain level crossings are sometimes fitted with strong lighting for the CCTV cameras with which the (remotely located) crossing keeper checks that the crossing is clear before lowering the barriers. Fitment of this equipment is not very likely in this part of the world; the speed radar detection equipment is also banned in many countries.

11 'Predictor' or Constant Warning Time Equipment

It was described earlier how in the USA the passing speed may differ greatly between freight and passenger trains and how as a result the waiting time between the start of the warning and the passage of the trains differs considerably. It is also known that the longer road users sit waiting at a level crossing, the more certain it is that they will start crossing against the warning, possibly assuming that the level crossing has failed. In order to counter this behaviour by shortening the waiting time until a train appears at the crossing, Constant Warning Time Equipment, sometimes marketed as 'Predictor', was developed. The basic function of this equipment is to ensure that from the moment the warning to the road users starts, the train will be at the crossing in a guaranteed short time span whatever the speed of the train.

What Constant Warning Time Equipment does is track the speed of the train and then calculate how long it will take to reach the point where the warning sequence at the crossing must be started to ensure the pre-determined time lapse between start of the warning and arrival of the train at the crossing. In the USA the experiences with this equipment are positive, except in a case such as the accident at Bourbonnais in March 1999. Here the positive effect of Constant Warning Time was undermined by a large number of slow pull-out-and-set-back marshalling movements over the level crossing.

For European circumstances this system has as yet not found great approval. Electrification with its return currents in the track combined with automatic signalling controlled by track circuits does not appear to work very well with this system. The European Train Control System, now being installed on various networks, has at its level 2 and 3 applications the ability to attach a Constant Warning Time function for level-crossing operation.

12 In-cab CCTV equipment for train drivers coupled to cameras on crossings

Following the Ufton Nervet accident (see Chapter 8) the train drivers' unions in Britain asked for equipment that would show the driver of a train approaching a level crossing whether the crossing surface is clear. If it all works properly and reliably probably not a bad solution, although the author's main concern is that it adds another item to the already considerable amount of equipment asking for attention in the cab and so takes away further attention from the track ahead. Additionally, for reasons of distraction, train drivers in Britain are no longer allowed to use telecommunications equipment while the train is moving and I feel that adding closed circuit television to the mix in the cab is defeating that object somewhat.

Point of view from the cab

From 10 years' experience as a train driver in southern Britain and through travelling in the cabs of many colleagues elsewhere in the world, the author thinks he is justified in stating that train drivers instinctively prefer the safety of those level crossings with barriers that must be closed well ahead of the approaching train and that are secured with interlocked signals.

If the crossing isn't properly closed the signals will not let the train reach it.

If the signals let the train through then the crossing is closed.

He is well aware that road users wait longer at the barriers of these crossings, but it is the belt- and braces-safety mode for all concerned.

Especially when driving a train at night, it is unpleasant to approach an automatic level crossing at speed, seeing the barriers come down only when there is no longer any chance at all to intervene if things go wrong. From the cab of a train, an AHB level crossing often gives the impression of closing when you're only yards away.

Naturally, nothing ever went wrong. As indicated throughout this book, the automatic level crossing is normally safe and accidents are rare.

APPENDIX A

THE EAST SUFFOLK LINE IS SAVED FROM CLOSURE

The East Suffolk line runs broadly from Ipswich to Lowestoft, but the main part of the line runs from Westerfield Junction, about four miles from Ipswich (where a line turns off to Felixstowe), to Oulton Broad North Junction (where it joins the line from Norwich), 1½ miles from Lowestoft.

In 1981 the economics of the line were so bad that complete closure was being seriously considered. The line was 43 miles long and had five signalboxes, 20 manned level crossings, one AHB crossing and 22 user-worked crossings. Passenger traffic was quite light and mainly local in character and there were eight intermediate stations, none of more than modest size. There was a short single-line branch from Saxmundham to Sizewell Power Station.

Fortunately, two developments unconnected with the East Suffolk line came to its rescue. A few years earlier a blizzard on the Highland line north from Inverness had caused considerable damage to the overhead telegraph line, and the cost of restoring it was so great that consideration was being given to complete closure of the line. The question was then raised as to whether radio communication could avoid the need to restore the telegraph route, and the Radio Electronic Token System was born, under which instructions to drivers were given directly by radio from a control centre.

Secondly, the 1978 Review of Level Crossing Protection had made some changes to the automatic open crossing locally monitored (AOCL) system, which made such crossings particularly appropriate to the requirements of the East Suffolk line. The signalling and the level crossings were then completely modernised, and a Radio Control Centre was established in the signalbox at Saxmundham, controlling trains on the whole line from Westerfield to Oulton Broad South. All the other signalboxes were closed. Today the line has 12 AOCL crossings, 11 ABCL crossings, one miniature red/green lights crossing, one manually-controlled barrier crossing (Saxmundham) and one AHB crossing. The ABCL crossing is a fairly recent development and is in effect an AOCL crossing with short barriers to reduce accidental misuse of the crossing by road users.

A series of photographs featuring some of the crossings on the line before modernisation. All were taken by the Stanley Hall in June 1981 during a review of the line held jointly with Inspecting Officers of the Railway Inspectorate.

Below: Two crossings close together, at Sun Wharf and Lime Kiln, Woodbridge.

Left: Saxmundham station now controls the whole line by radio and still works the level crossing, which now has lifting barriers. This is the view south towards Ipswich, the remains of the down platform being discernible beyond the crossing gates.

Below: A view of Westhall Crossing, between Halesworth and Brampton, showing the crossing keeper's cottage.

Above: Brampton Crossing.

Right: London Road Crossing,
Beccles.

Above and left: Two views of Weston Crossing, north of Brampton.

Level Crossings

Right: Ingate Street Crossing, Beccles.

Below: Grove Road Crossing, Beccles.

APPENDIX B

ACTS OF PARLIAMENT AND OTHER OFFICIAL DOCUMENTS

Highways Act 1835
Highway (Railway Crossings) Act 1839
Regulation of Railways Act 1842
Railways Clauses Consolidation Act 1845
Malicious Damage Act 1861
Railways Clauses Act 1863
Regulation of Railways Act 1871
Road Traffic Act 1930
Road & Rail Traffic Act 1933
British Transport Commission Act 1954
British Transport Commission Act 1957
Level Crossing Protection Report (HMSO) 1957

Highways Act 1959
Road Traffic Regulation Act 1967
Transport Act 1968
Road Traffic Act 1972
Traffic Signs, Regulations and General Directions 1975 (HMSO)
Level Crossing Protection Report 1978 (HMSO)
Railway Construction and Operation requirements — Level Crossings 1981 (HMSO)
Level Crossings Act 1983
Railway Safety Principles and Guidance — Level Crossings 1996 (HSE)

ACKNOWLEDGEMENTS AND BIBLIOGRAPHY

Acknowledgements

Peter van Der Mark is especially grateful for the support rendered by the following people and organisations:

Jim Vine, friend and BR Southern Region traction engineer with a vast knowledge about everything railway who gave me a thorough grounding in basic rail safety principles, traction and operations before passing away in June 2002.

Wim Coenraad, signalling engineer and friend, whom I owe especially for his valuable leisure time, spent checking manuscripts and looking up pictures for this book.

Erich Preuß, respected writer on rail safety and operations in Germany.

Frans van de Water and his staff in the level crossing department of Prorail, the State railway infrastructure provider in the Netherlands.

Hans van Hiel and his colleagues at NedTrain Consulting (now Lloyd's Register Rail Consultancy) who gave detailed information on obstacle deflectors.

Henk Wijnmalen at Vialis Railway Safety Systems, for photographs of their work in parts of the world you normally wouldn't really think of going to.

And, last but not least, **Alison Forster**, my boss at the time, for allowing me to write and publish freely.

Bibliography

International books and magazines

Much information was taken from the internet; informative sites are those of the various transport safety boards in the world, many publishing in English next to their national language. There are many international railway magazines that provide information about railway accidents of all kinds. The most important books and reports were:

Editions Flohic: *Le Patrimoine de la SNCF et des Chemins de Fer Français*, tome II, deuxième édition
    ISBN 2-84234-084-1

Erich Preuß: *Eisenbahnunfälle in Europa*. Berlin 1991
    ISBN 3-334-70716-7

Erich Preuß: *Kursbuch des Schreckens*. Stuttgart 1998
    ISBN 3-613-71093-5

ESCAP (UN): *Evaluation of cost-effective systems for railway level crossing protection*. New York 2000
    ST/ESCAP/2088

IRSE project group, ed Colin Bailey: *European Railway Signalling*. London 1995
    ISBN 0-7136-4167-3

LJP Albers & JC de Jongh: *Van Stoom naar Nieuwe Stijl*. Amsterdam 1970
    ISBN 90-6054-659-8

New York State Comptroller (Alan G. Hevesi): *Safety of Grade-Level Railroad Crossings 2004-S-63*

Peter Semmens: *Railway Disasters of the World*. Sparkford 1994 ISBN 1-85260-323-2

Projectgroep VVO, ed Drs E. Griffioen: *Final report Improving Level Crossing Safety*. Railned Spoorveiligheid, Utrecht 1999. Original Dutch text, my English translation minus artwork available as an electronic file (also the follow-on observation reports on the effectivity of the measures proposed)

Queensland University of Technology, Australia. Human Factors at Railway Level Crossings: Key Issues and Target Road User Groups

Queensland University of Technology, Australia. *Motorist Behaviour at Railway Level Crossings: An exploratory study of train driver experience*

Rob & Marcel van Ee: *Ongevallen op het Nederlands Spoor*. Alkmaar 1997 ISBN 90-6013-067-7

Robert C. Reed: *Train Wrecks*. Bonanza Books, New York, LCCC 68-13249

Schneider & Masé: *Katastrophen auf Schienen*. Zürich 1968

Stanley Hall: *Modern Signalling Handbook* revised 3rd edition 2005 ISBN 0-7110-3143-6

Staysafe Committee (Australia):

1) Report on the safety of railway level crossings 4/53 October 2004

2) Progress in improving the safety of railway level crossings 24/53 December 2006

British books and magazines

Bigg, James (editor), *Clauses Consolidation Acts 1845-1864*, Waterlow & Sons (1866)

Jacobs, Gerald (editor), *Railway Track Diagrams*, Quail Track Diagrams (various dates)

James, Leslie, BA LLB FCIT, *The Law of the Railway*, Barry Rose (Publishers) Ltd (1980)

Board of Trade/Ministry of Transport (and similar departmental titles)

Railway Accident reports to the Secretary of State for Transport (and various titles) on the Safety Record of the Railways in Great Britain during the year, issued annually by HMSO (latterly by HSE, then subsequently by other public bodies)

Other official reports as listed in Appendix B 'Acts of Parliament and other Official Documents'

Individual accident reports by the Officers of the Railway Inspectorate (various dates) HMSO

Report of the Public Inquiry into the Accident at Hixon level crossing on 6 January 1968 (HMSO) Cmnd 3706 (known as the Gibbens Report)

Reports

'Accident Reports' – reports to the Secretary of State for Transport (and various titles) on the Safety Record of the Railways in Great Britain during the year, issued annually by HMSO (latterly by HSE, then subsequently by other public bodies)

Individual accident reports by the Officers of the Railway Inspectorate (various dates), HMSO

Report of the Public Inquiry into the Accident at Hixon level crossing on 6 January 1968 (HMSO) Cmnd 3706 (known as the Gibbens Report)

Level Crossing Protection Report, 1957 (HMSO)

Traffic Signs, Regulations and General Directions, 1975 (HMSO)

Level Crossing Protection Report, 1978 (HMSO)

Railway Construction and Operation Requirements – Level Crossings, 1981 (HMSO)

Railway Safety Principles and Guidance – Level Crossings, 1996 (HSE)